BR   Fogde, Myron Jean,
525   1934-
.F63
        The church goes West

DATE			
NOV 0 1 1998			

FAITH
OF OUR
FATHERS

VOLUME SIX

The Church Goes West

Myron Jean Fogde

A Consortium Book

Library of Congress Card Catalog Number: 77-74856
ISBN: 0-8434-0625-9

ACKNOWLEDGEMENT

O.E. Rolvaag, GIANTS IN THE EARTH. New York, Harper and Row,
Publishers, 1927, 1929. Used with permission.

Dedicated to my wife, Lois,
and our children Stephen and Susan

Table of Contents

1

Theological Currents

During the decades preceding the Civil War, the denomi-national form of voluntary associations with its concomitant pattern of competing congregations and national bodies had become the accepted form of ecclesiastical organization in the United States; and for the fifty years that followed there was to be no measureable alteration in this pattern. However, the theological content, the bulk of which these competing religious organizations shared in common, was to move about in a number of directions so that organizational form remained stable while theological content varied considerably.

An examination of this theological variety must be seen in the context of the scene in the immediate post-Civil War era. A widely accepted analysis suggests "that the United States, in effect, had two religions, or at least two different forms of the same religion, and that the prevailing Protestant ideology represented a syncretistic mingling of the two."[1] The first of these was "the religion of the denominations, which was commonly articulated in the terms of scholastic Protestant orthodoxy and almost universally practiced in terms of the experimental religion of pietistic revivalism."[2] The second form that prevailed simultaneously was "the religion of the democratic society and nation. This was rooted in the rationalism of the Enlightenment (to go no farther back) and was articulated in terms of the destiny of America, under God, to

3

be fulfilled by perfecting the democratic way of life for the example and betterment of all mankind."[3]

In this land where Thomas Jefferson's "fair experiment" in religious freedom, including the separation of church and state, was apparently successful, the accent was on the religious decision and obligation of the individual. In such a personalized religion, the historic role of the sacraments and the influence of systematic theology were significantly reduced. At first in the North, which thought of itself as enjoying Divine vindication for upholding the great moral truths in the recent civil strife, and then later in the South as well, these same Christians were eager to join in the rapid development of the country and to enjoy the attendant material blessings. While theology seemed to be going bankrupt, individual commitment to a religious as well as economic and social struggle came to the fore, all thought of as being part of God's grand design for the favored land.

This provided an environment conducive to theological inquiry on the part of those who wished to take the time to do so, and there were indeed those who did, who sought to undergird their faith in a rapidly changing world by a substantive and creative theological foundation. Many, of course, could not understand such an endeavor, and in giving lip service to the statements of the past were too busy living what they thought to be practical Christian lives to have much concern for these new endeavors; that is, until they saw in them serious challenges to their accustomed ways. Then the placid waters of theological quietude were at times roiled; and in the ensuing conflicts more heat than light was often generated. As the religious scene became polarized, the pious faithful often wondered what all the clamour was about as they in their own personal ways continued to nurture their Christian lives.

The problem, however, arose initially in the South, for how was the Christian, who was convinced that God had indeed sanctioned slavery, to satisfactorily explain to him-

self the terrible judgment that had befallen him and his beloved land? He could not accept the reasoning of Henry Ward
Beecher of Brooklyn, who declared: "this continent is to be
cared for by the North simply because the North has been
true to the cause of Christ in...a sufficient measure to secure
her own safety;...and the nation is to be given to us because
we have the bosom by which to nourish it." The Southerner
did explain it otherwise, and in spite of the enormous physical and emotional desolation, the Civil War did not destroy
the South's religious tradition, but actually rejuvenated this
unique understanding of Western Christianity and preserved
its existence for at least another century. This was accomplished by the continuance of the dominant Methodist and
Baptist denominations. The Southern Methodist Church now
came to think of itself as the custodian of the Lost Cause, and
by a series of revivals quickly won back the dominant place
in Southern life that it had enjoyed in antebellum days. The
Baptists, even more than the Methodists, did not come to
terms with the intellectual currents of the time and were
hampered in doing so by agrarian backwardness and educational deficiencies. As a result the denomination became
more and more parochial, and the individual Baptist congregations came to reflect without criticism the ideas and mores
of their local members. The peculiar institutions of the South
were thus propagandized as the will of God by new forms of
segregation that more completely divided the races then they
had been before. Continuing to rely on the influence of the
perennial revivals, Christian development also came to be
associated with particular personal mores emphasizing the
avoidance of tobacco, gambling, theatergoing, card playing,
dancing, and especially drinking according to as strict a code
as had been previously held. Because of these trends the denominations grew rapidly with the Baptists by 1906 replacing
the Methodists as the largest church in the South. The situation within these dominant churches as well as in the other denominations remained largely unchanged into the twentieth

century, and with their predominantly rural and small-town constituency these churches were the upholders of social patterns and ways of thought that were increasingly anachronistic in the nation at large. It has been concluded that "their significance in Southern life consisted not in their power to mold their environment...[but] in supporting and perpetuating the standards prevailing in society at large."4 Thus, in the heyday of Jim Crow, the white Protestant churches overwhelmingly remained a mainstay of support for the Southern cause.

The story in the South is not, however, only the history of the churches expressing the convictions of the white citizens. When the Emancipation Proclamation was issued in 1863, a half million of the four million Blacks that were freed had some degree of affiliation with Protestant Churches, also primarily the Methodist and Baptist. Within a very short time most of these Christianized Blacks withdrew from the white churches, and thus an even wider field for evangelization opened. Quickly Black churches appeared to fill the void, and it is no wonder when statements such as made in the Richmond *Religious Herald* in 1869 were common sentiment: "to admit Negroes into churches on an equal basis would lead to the mongrelization of our noble Anglo-Saxon race."

The Colored Primitive Baptists were organized in 1866 and also in that year the first all Negro state convention of regular Baptists was organized in North Carolina. With the ease with which Baptist churches can be organized, countless independent Black Baptist churches arose, leading many, but by no means all, to form the National Baptist Convention in 1895. In fact, the Baptist churches came to dominate the Black Christian scene. Among other denominations was the formulation of the Colored Cumberland Presbyterian Church in 1869 to be followed a few years later by the Colored Presbyterian Church from the major Southern Presbyterian body. It was the Methodists, next to the Baptists, who were the best prepared to organize Black churches, and in 1866 the Southern Methodists released their Black members to form the Colored Methodist Episcopal Church while the invading Northern Methodists created a separate Negro Conference within their national body. More successful in gaining members for Methodism were two previously organized Black churches that had been active in the North since early in the nineteenth century: the African Methodist Episcopal Church and the African Methodist Episcopal Church Zion, together claiming by 1900 some 800,000 members of the Black church membership that stood at 2.7 million in a total Black population of 8.3 million. By 1916, over forty per cent of the Blacks in America were members of Christian denominations, a percentage comparable to that of the white population.

This rapid growth of the Black churches gives ample evidence that the religion they proclaimed did provide acceptable answers to the deeply felt needs of the freedmen for whom freedom frequently had not been a glorious release. With the coming of Jim Crow laws, intimidation and political suppression the little congregations meeting in simple wooden buildings became the chief means of creating and developing a structured social life among the freedmen; and did so on the foundational basis of belief and piety that had been and continued to be integral to Southern Protestantism, whether expressed in a white or Black church. For among the Blacks as well, the faith was expressed in a common anti-intellectualism and based on a strict moral code that was preached in the perennial revival. Much of this may have been a personal escapism from the dismal surroundings that both Blacks and whites experienced. It must be observed that the Black churches did not have much of a social gospel emphasis and so did not seek to correct the abuses in the social system; but instead they accepted the social scene and sought to articulate an individual salvation in the world to come as had already long been expressed in the Negro Spiritual. Nonetheless, the Black churches did seek to fulfil many of the social needs of the Black population.

Leading these Black congregations was the dominant figure of the Black preacher, who was also frequently the leader of the entire Black community. A noted observer of the scene states the case this way: "In the Baptist Churches in which the majority of the Negroes have always been concentrated there was even greater opportunity for self-assertion, and the assumption of leadership on the part of strong men. This naturally resulted in a pattern of autocratic leadership which has spilled over into most aspects of organized social life among Negroes."[5] During the Reconstruction Era, the Black preacher could also find an outlet for his leadership abilities in the political arena, but after the re-establishment of white supremacy in the South he was forced to make the church his arena of political activity. Not only the preacher but the members as well found in the church their only real outlet for the practice of politics, and for generations the local congregation was the scene of such political activity as the white population could practice in the civil life of society.

One of the major social tasks confronting the church was the development of Black family life. This had been almost destroyed during the period of slavery, so much so that it was no longer among the mores of the Blacks to live the monogamous style. Black churches became active agents in the re-establishment of this practice among the freedmen, but it was a difficult task. Economic co-operation was another area of activity which began when Blacks pooled their very meager resources to build the little churches, and this soon evolved into mutual aid societies to meet such crises in life as sickness and death, and then at times branched out into various enterprises. In the area of education the denominations also took a leading role. Northern mission societies and churches sent funds and staff to establish schools for the Blacks, prominent among which was the largely Congregational American Missionary Association. In working with the Freedmen's Bureau, created by an Act of Congress in 1865, public schools and colleges were founded that provided Black leadership in the generations to follow. Also the Black churches themselves made efforts at establishing schools, but this was a difficult task as they did not have an intellectual tradition and were often hostile to such a development. Yet schools were established by outside forces or on the basis of local initiative and were permeated with a religious and moral outlook whatever their academic shortcomings.

So it was that the Black church sought to care for the Black under the conditions in which he lived. As has been written: "The Negro church with its own forms of religious worship was a world which the white man did not invade but only regarded with an attitude of condescending amusement. The Negro church could enjoy this freedom so long as it offered no threat to the white man's dominance in both economic and social relations. And, on the whole, the Negro's church was not a threat to white domination and aided the Negro to become accommodated to an inferior status. The religion of the Negro continued to be other-worldly in its outlook, dismissing the privations and sufferings and injustices of this world as temporary and transient... [but] he could always find an escape from such, often painful, experiences within the shelter of his church."6 The editor of the *Christian Recorder* of Philadelphia commended the Black church when he wrote in 1913: "The Negro church is the only Protestant church in America which has kept hold of the common laborer, and it is the largest and strongest organization among Negroes."

In the South as in the nation at large in the decades immediately following the Civil War, the Protestant faith, in spite of its denominational variations, was coming to have increasing dominance in the nation's culture, even as this meant being closely identified with that culture. It is therefore to be expected that theological thinking would shift as the basis of the culture changed; and change for many it did. Turning to the Northern states, the uncritically accepted supernaturalism of religious tradition became challenged following the Civil War by the advent of scientific thinking that initially centered around the concept of evolution, and this indeed for some forced a re-examination of the intellectual foundations of religious thinking. As has been noted: "Evolutionism forced the denominations to take up again the intellectual business laid on the table at the opening of the nineteenth century and largely ignored during the intervening busy years of institutional proliferation and growth."[7] The results of this catalytic agent to theological inquiry were diverse.

It was the writings of the Englishman, Charles Darwin, whose *Origin of Species* (1859), and *The Descent of Man* (1871), now forced the confrontation between scientific and religious thought. One of the American defenders of the insights for religion that were implied in Darwin was Lyman Abbott, successor to Henry Ward Beecher at Plymouth Church in Brooklyn, who in 1897 stated in his *Theology of an Evolutionist*: "Evolution does not attempt to explain the origin of life. It is simply a history of the process of life. With the secret cause of life evolution has nothing to do." Stating this more positively, Abbott wrote: "Evolution is, broadly speaking, the doctrine of growth applied to life; the doctrine that all life proceeds in a natural and normal progress from lower to higher stages, from simpler to more complex stages, and by a vital force or forces operating from without."

Taking these deductions from scientific observation, Abbot then studied the history of the human race as he traced it through the Bible, the history of civilizations and as he observed it in his own time, and concluded that the same movement of progress is to be seen. Thus he could join with John Fiske and unabashedly proclaim: "Evolution is God's Way of doing things." To those who shared this perspective, theology must then be about the business of keeping pace with progress; and Abbott explained it this way: "So there is a new theology, though not a new religion. God, sin, repentance, forgiveness, love, remain essentially unchanged, but the definitions of God, sin, repentance, forgiveness, and love are changed from generation to generation. There is as little danger of undermining religion by new definitions of theology as there is of blotting out the stars from the heavens by a new astronomy. But as religion is the life of God in the soul of man, definitions which give to man a clearer and a more intelligible understanding of that life will promote it, and definitions which are, or seem to be irrational, will tend to impede or impair it." A theological renaissance was now to succeed the scientific renaissance, and the end result of this according to Abbott is "that the resurrection I regard as a fact; evolution as a theory...the latest word and the best word of science, but not necessarily its last or final word." In thus placing himself squarely on the traditional central belief of Christianity, he can show what developments evolutionary thinking has made in increasing the Christian's appropriation of the mind of God. The Christian evolutionist "believes in redemption, not as a restoration to a lost state of innocence, impossible to be restored, but as a culmination of the long process when man shall be presented before his Father without spot or wrinkle or blemish or any such thing. He believes, not propitiation of an angry God by Another suffering to appease the Father's wrath, but in the perpetual self-propitiation of the Father, whose mercy, going forth to redeem from sin, satisfies, as nothing else could, the divine indignation against sin by abolishing it. He believes in immortality, not as a mere endless existence, but as an undying nature, which is superior to death, because it shares with God, its Redeemer, the power of an endless life. And he believes in religion, not as a creed, a ritual, or a church order, but as self-control, righteousness, reverence, hope, love,— the life of God in the soul of man." Here was one prominent American preacher that was convinced that the insights provided by Darwinian thought enhanced the Christian's understanding of the course of human history as well as the maturing of his own life.

It was not only in the realm of theological thought that Darwinian thought was applied. Influential in accommodating Darwin quickly to the economic and social dimensions of latter nineteenth century American life were Herbert Spencer and William Graham Sumner with their propagandizing of Social Darwinism. In the using of such popular catchwords in Darwin as "struggle for existence" and "survival of the fittest" by those who triumphed in the economic competition of the rapidly industrializing America, Darwinism soon became one of the great informing insights in the history of the conservative mind in America because such concepts gave the force of natural law to the idea of competitive struggle that so marked the economic scene.

While the theological implications of Darwinism called for a revamping of an uncritical acceptance of traditional theology, the social and economic implications were at once seen as foundational to the ideology already permeating American society. Then by the opening of the twentieth century the individualistic aspect of Darwinism came to be replaced in the minds of some by its concept of the organic whole. Thus Darwinism could now be championed by those who challenged the prevelant rugged individualism, and who instead sought to bring a social consciousness to bear upon the enormous problems confronting the American laborer.

Darwinism was capable of being quoted on both sides of the economic and social fence, and among the conservative religious majority this also caused consternation. "Darwinism intensified the uncertainties which succeeded rapid social change, while rapid social change exaggerated the threat of Darwinism."[8] For these conservatives "the ultimate security which Darwinism attacked was felt to be the final security in a world where basic values were crumbling. That much of the fear was inarticulate and many of the relations unperceived does not minimize the reality of the total situation."[9]

Although the issue that first rose to the surface and remained there was the alleged atheism of Darwinism, this became muted, when it was demonstrated that Darwinism need not be concerned with the creation of man, but only his development. However, the statement of Darwin vividly portraying man's ancestor as "a hairy quadruped, furnished with a tail and pointed ears, probably arboreal in habits" did not in any way allay the fear that Darwinism led inevitably to a final denial of man being created in the image of God. As potent a possibility as this was, it was not the most serious challenge that anti-Darwinians would not yield; this was the issue of the nature of the Bible. Darwinian revelations came at the same time that European Biblical scholars were suggesting that the Bible itself was the result of a long development of oral and written traditions, including history, folklore, discourses, poetry and prophecy brought together over a period of more than a thousand years. The question was well put by Washington Gladden in the title of an 1891 book: *Who Wrote the Bible*, appearing just a decade after a revised version of the King James Bible was published in 1881 and 1885 using some of the insights of this new study. This British and American enterprise was followed in 1901 by the American Standard Edition incorporating further changes sought by the American scholars. Again it was Lyman Abbott who popularized a combination of Darwinism and higher criticism in Biblical scholarship when he wrote: "The modern Christian evolutionist believes that revelation has been made in this manner to the world: that God has inspired men in their quest for truth, and that under inspiration, studying, meditating, and laboring, they find their way to the truth." Then he could say that "to him the Bible is a collection of literature, containing in a preeminent measure the growth of the consciousness of God in the human soul, as interpreted by the preeminent religious leaders of a preeminently religious people." Then as regard the role of science he stated: "The descriptions of nature which it contains are scientifically inaccurate; but they are written by men who saw God in nature and interpreted nature as itself an interpreter of

God." Abbott saw the issue here not as merely a question of dates and authorship—as to whether Moses wrote the Pentateuch or not, how many Psalms were written by David or whether or not there were two Isaiahs, or even the questions arising about the character of the gospel narratives in regard to the historical life of Jesus. He insisted that a profoundly serious issue was at stake here and that the new treatment of the Scriptures was indeed revolutionary. He likened it to the sixteenth century reformation when he declared that the new Biblical scholarship "denies the infallibility of the Bible as the Protestant reformation denied the infallibility of the Church." Then leaving that comparison he goes on to declare: "There is no infallible authority. Infallible authority is undesirable. God has not given it to His children. He has given them something far better,—life. That life can come only through struggle.... The Bible is the record of the experiences of devout men struggling toward that knowledge of God which is life eternal; it is given to us, not to save us from struggle, and growth by struggle, but to inspire us to struggle that we may grow."

Here the battle was joined. One of the most temperate in his conservative stance was the evangelist Dwight L. Moody. He told of an incident where a man in following his minister's sermons carefully cut out of a Bible whatever the minister said was not authentic. One day the man visited his pastor and brought with him the expurgated Bible, and the following conversation reputedly took place:

"Here, Pastor is your Bible."

"My Bible?" said the clergyman impatiently.

"Yes; I have cut out all that you say is fable and allegory and folklore and also the mythical and so-called inauthentic parts, and here is what is left."

"Give it to me," said the preacher.

"No, you don't," the man replied. "You haven't touched the covers yet, and I am going to cling to them at least."

Moody's comment to this scene was typical of this generous, but conservative man: "I believe that there are a good many scholars in these days, as there were when St. Paul lived, 'who, professing themselves to be wise, have become fools'; but I don't think they are those who hold to the inspiration of the Bible. I have said that ministers of the Gospel who are cutting up the Bible in this way, denying Moses today and Isaiah tomorrow, and Daniel the next day and Jonah the next, are doing great injury to the church; and I stand by what I have said. I don't say that they are bad men. They may be good men, but that makes the results of their work all the worse. Do they think they will recommend the Bible to the finite and fallen reason of men by taking the supernatural out of it? They are doing just the opposite. They are emptying the churches and driving the young men of this generation to infidelity." To Moody the real problem was not the question of two Isaiahs but a lack of familiarity with the prophecy itself. The Biblical studies for intellectual gain did not disturb him, but the undermining of the faith of the masses of people did; and it was on this basis of practicality, plus his own conservative bent, that he clung to the traditional belief in regard to the inspiration of the Scriptures.

Not so compassionate for the scholar was the flamboyant evangelist, Billy Sunday, who thundered away: "I don't believe in the bastard theory of evolution. If you believe your great granddaddy had a tail and was a monkey, take your old long-tailed ancestors and go to the devil." On another occasion he could spout forth: "I don't know any more about theology than a jack rabbit does about ping-pong—I don't know any more about theology than a whale does about crochet work—but I do know what true repentance is." While Moody had a sympathy with intellectual inquiry, though he did not use the results himself as he thought they were not aiding his cause, Sunday a generation later had succumbed to an efficiency based on entertainment gimmicks and the Bible came for him to have the simply utilitarian value that led him to say: "I believe the Bible is the word of God from cover to cover. I believe that the man who magnifies the word of God in his preaching is the man whom God will honor." This was shouting down the challenge, not meeting it on its own grounds of academic study.

Two of the men to spearhead the drive to academically challenge the new studies were the venerable father and son Princeton professors Charles and Alexander Hodge. In an article published in 1881, Alexander Hodge and Benjamin Warfield defined and defended the doctrine of inspiration which they said was "the superintendence by God of the writers in the entire process of their writing, which accounts for nothing whatever but the absolute infallibility of the record in which the revelation, once generated, appears in the original autograph. "From this basis they could then conclude: "we are sincerely convinced of the perfect soundness of the great Catholic doctrine of Biblical Inspiration, i.e., that the Scriptures not only contain, but ARE THE WORD OF GOD, and hence that all their elements and all their affirmations are absolutely errorless, and binding the faith and obedience of men." Nonetheless, they insisted that this be established on the basis of rigorous academic study, realizing of course the fallibility of human methods of study and the faulty translations of the original text down through the centuries. These writers claimed not to be expostulating the concept of verbal dictation, but rather that God superintended the writers, who, while acting spontaneously, wrote their own ideas in their own way while they recorded revelation and other matters. This controversy came to be an important ingredient in the conservative development which came to be known in the 1920's as "Fundamentalism," and which became a raging controversy in some denominations during that decade.

Hodge and Warfield were careful not to overplay this one issue, regardless of how important it did seem to many. They pointed out that "inspiration can have no meaning if Christianity is not true, but Christianity would be true and divine, and being so, would stand, even if God had not been pleased to give us, in addition to His revelation of saving truth, an infallible record of that revelation absolutely errorless, by means of Inspiration." Inspiration was, however, there; and on the basis of this infallibility, compromised only a little by the faulty texts available, there was to gradually emerge in American conservative religious thought a rational fundamentalism that was to use the art of logic to develop and prove systematic theologies founded on the given Scriptural text. This was at times like the scientist who observes, arranges, and systematizes, but does not participate in his experiment.

One of the areas in which this had been done, even prior to the advent of Darwin, was in the creation story. Geologists, such as Sir Charles Lyall, had scientifically demonstrated that the earth was millions of years old. Sensing this as a direct threat to the Biblical record of the six days of creation many vociferously denounced the geologists. Others used Scriptural texts such as "a thousand years in Thy sight are but as yesterday" to reinterpret the word "day" in the Genesis account to mean "eon," thus preserving the literalness of the Biblical account as buttressed by new insights. While this was satisfactory to some, it was not to others. Recognizing this, Charles Hodge stated: "We can even afford to acknowledge our incompetence to meet them in argument, or to anwer their objections; and yet our faith remains unshaken and rational." Wide dissemination of an attempt to intellectually promote the conservative cause is seen in the publication of twelve small volumes, collectively known as *The Fundamentals: A Testimony to the Truth* from 1909 to 1915. Financed by two wealthy Los Angeles laymen, these books were sent free of charge to every pastor, evangelist, missionary, theological student, Sunday school superintendent, YMCA and YWCA secretary, totaling some three million copies. One of the editors, Amzi Dixon, insisted that there could be no reconciliation between religious and scientific thought, and also maintained that there could be no religious revival apart from commitment to the inspiration and infallible authority of the Scripture. In the volumes there was a heavy emphasis on Biblical proof texts and literalism, but also a pervading piety which brings to the fore personal testimonies at the conclusion of several of the books. Numerous articles on Higher Criticism, and especially how this affects the Pentateuch, are prominent; but many topics are discussed, such as the deity of Christ, the Virgin Birth, bodily resurrection, and the atonement as positive statements, together with articles on Darwinism, Mormonism, Eddyism and Romanism. The last volume was devoted to evangelism, once again underscoring the piety of the series. The thrust of the point of view contained in the volumes had been discussed in a series of Bible conferences that had begun at Niagara Falls in 1876 and at a number of prophetic and premillennial conferences which had begun two years later as a result of the earlier meetings.

In the midst of the rigidifying of the conservative forces occurred a number of professorial dismissals as a result of a series of heresy trials that affected primarily the Presbyterian Church, though also others to a lesser extent. Wide publicity was given to the case of Dr. Charles A. Briggs, Professor of Biblical Theology at Union Seminary in New York. In 1891, when he took that position, he delivered an address entitled: "The Authority of Holy Scripture," in which he sharply criticized the doctrine of the inerrancy of the Bible. For this he was accused of being a heretic according to the norm of the Presbyterian Church, and after a tortuous route through the denomination's judicatories was suspended from the ministry in 1893. The seminary then severed its tenuous relations with the denomination and became an independent theological school, with Briggs remaining on the faculty and receiving priest's orders in the Episcopal Church in 1899. Another case involved Professor Henry Preserved

Smith of Lane Seminary in Cincinnati, who after attacking the doctrine of verbal inspiration in 1891 was suspended from the ministry by the Presbytery of Cincinnati, with this action being sustained by the General Assembly of the Church. He then became a Congregationalist. Another noted case involved Arthur C. McGiffert, who resigned from the Presbyterian ministry in 1900 so that a trial was avoided.

Other denominations, while not involved so much in the formal condemnations of professors were also torn by controversy; yet it must be remembered that few of the rank-and-file members of these churches were embroiled in these squabbles. What theological self-consciousness they had was conservative and traditional, but not rigidly so. Though they tended to have a tolerant spirit like D. L. Moody in regard to academic theological questions, they could be persuaded by the local minister, or develop a greater semblance of theological sophistication through such a Bible as the annotated C.I. Scofield Reference Bible which became available in 1909. This popular edition of the Scriptures imposed a rigid schematization on Biblical materials by relating each part of Scripture to a timetable of "dispensations" which were to climax in the second coming of Christ. Asserting a development in religion, the Scriptures were divided into seven periods of time, wherein was the basis whereby "God judged man not on an absolute and unchanging standard but according to ground rules especially devised for each dispensation." [10] For example, under the dispensation of Grace, which is the current age, men are required to repent and turn in faith to Christ; while under that of the Law, which existed from Abraham to Christ, men were commanded to obey the law. Based upon "a frozen biblical text in which every word was supported by the same weight of divine authority," [11] this dispensational theology embodied a religious faith that could be buttressed by a rational certitude.

In the midst of this theological strife, standing above it and seeking to pull their contemporaries to a higher spiritual level of life were a group of men, the pulpit princes of an age when oratorical skill could draw huge congregations. One of the mightiest of these was Henry Ward Beecher (1813-1887) who for forty years was the nation's most famous preacher at Plymouth Church in the quiet suburb of Brooklyn. Beecher summed up the values and ideals of his middle-class affluent congregation and the vast readership he enjoyed across the nation. He was not a creative thinker, but rather a popularizer, and has been characterized as "that magnificent weather vane of respectable opinion." [12]

Before the War Beecher had dramatized his opposition to slavery by "auctioning" slaves during worship in Plymouth Church, who were then freed. He had shown his opposition to the extension of slavery into "Bleeding Kansas" by urging men to go to this new territory to save the Great Plains from this horrible curse armed with rifles that he helped raise money to provide by his pulpit oratory. As some were shipped in boxes identified as "Bibles" they became known as "Beecher's Bibles." After the War he exuded the Divine vindication of the Northern cause, yet he did not support a vindictive attitude toward the South. He accompanied the American flag on its return to Fort Sumter saying: "If any man goes supposing that he accompanies me on an errand of triumph and exultation over a fallen foe, he does not know the first letter of my feelings." Rather he asserted that this act was a visible indication of his desire for the rapid re-entry of the Southern states into the Union since secession had been illegal. Hence he was a supporter of the program of President Johnson, though this stand put him in conflict with a large portion of his congregation and readership but underscored his tenacity to principle.

In the rapid industrial development that followed, Beecher came to be a firm advocate of the gospel of wealth. Concerning the masses being victimized by the industrial barons he had this word of judgment: "Looking comprehensively through city and town and village and country, the general truth will stand, that no man in this land suffers from poverty unless it be more than his fault—unless it be his sin.... There is enough and to spare thrice over; and if men have not enough, it is owing to the want of provident care, and foresight, and industry, and frugality, and wise saving. This is the general truth." Instead of groveling in poverty, a man should apply himself and rise, but in the meantime, not be destroyed by present circumstances. He gave this advice to railroad workers: "It is said that a dollar a day is not enough for a wife and five or six children. No, not if that man smokes or drinks beer. It is not enough if they are to live as he would be glad to have them live... But is not a dollar a day enough to buy bread with? Water costs nothing; and a man who cannot live on bread is not fit to live." This was not the only emphasis in the social thought of Beecher. With the Bible before him and citing it frequently, he did address the whole range of social questions, and while taking a conservative position himself, he laid the groundwork for his successor, Lyman Abbott, to take quite different stances and become a leading advocate of social programs that were being politically expounded by Theodore Roosevelt.

Also in the area of theology, Beecher attempted to mirror the trends of the time. He told the Yale Divinity School students in 1872: "If ministers do not make their theological systems conform to the facts as they are; if they do not recognize what men are studying, the time will not be far distant when the pulpit will be like a voice crying in the wilderness, And it will not be 'Prepare the way of the Lord,' either.... The providence of God is rolling forward in a spirit of investigation that Christian ministers must meet and join." Becoming a "cordial Christian evolutionist" Beecher sought, nevertheless, to be a fairly cautious pioneer in the new theologies that were developing. He desired to raise the insights of his hearers and readers, but he did not wish to outdistance them. He was concerned to remain within the bounds of their intellectual, religious and social tolerance.

It was his style that endeared him to his congregations. For the first ten years of his ministry he followed the revivalistic tradition of his father, Lyman Beecher, in two Indiana churches. He then came to the newly formed Plymouth Church, and through his versatility, vitality and wit exercised while standing on a stage that jutted out into the 2,500 seat auditorium he directly confronted the packed congregations that came to hear him causing them at times to laugh and at times to cry, but whatever the mode, he always sought to convince them of what he was saying.

Though he addressed a multitude of social and political topics, he subsumed them under his theological picture of God's love for the sinner, which was not based on some idea of election or a covenant, but "from the fullness of his great heart." This perspective he articulated as he recalled his conversion experience:

> when it pleased God to reveal to my wandering soul the idea that it was his nature to love a man in his sins for the sake of helping him out of them; that he did not do it out of compliment to Christ, or to a law, or a plan of salvation, but from the fullness of his great heart; that he was a Being not made mad by sin, but sorry; that he was not furious with wrath toward the sinner, but pitied him—in short that he felt toward me as my mother felt toward me, to whose eyes my wrongdoing brought tears, who never pressed me so close to her as when I had done wrong, and who would fain with her yearning love lift me out of trouble....when I found that it was Christ's nature to lift men out of meakness to strength, out of impurity to goodness, out of everything low and debasing to superiority, I felt that I had found a God.

Beecher looked forward optimistically to the development of the Kingdom of God in America. At times being charged with preaching "a kind of qualitative hedonism,"[13] and of letting edification give way to entertainment, Beecher did portray religion as a natural experience, and something for everyday use, as well as something to be enjoyed. His admirers saw him as a man with a hearty, joyous nature, touching human life at every point. His successor and biographer, Lyman Abbott, stated of his preaching: "He believed in the potential divinity in every man; he believed that if this potential divinity were once awakened and given its true place, it would bring all the man into subjection to the law of God, and he sought by reason, by imagination, by humour, by pathos, by illustration, and by emotion, but yet more than any of these, by direct spiritual contact, to evoke this divine potentiality and make it actual and effective." He went on to observe that Beecher "recognized God's fellowship in all the common experiences of life. This pervasive faith made him not merely an orator about religion, but an imparter of religion, and this constituted the secret of his pulpit power. It interprets at once his real reverence and his seeming irreverance; his fellowship with God no less in secular than in sacred hours, and his disregard for the conventions of religion."

Even a protracted civil suit concerning his alleged indiscretions with a Mrs. Elizabeth Tilden, from which he was finally partially exonerated by a split jury, did not destroy his effectiveness. His sermons after 1859 were published in *The Plymouth Pulpit*, and successive volumes of sermons and lectures received nationwide distribution; even major secular newspapers printed his sermons in full. Others had to prepare them for print, as they were delivered extemporaneously with only a few notes before him. Nonetheless, they were thoroughly prepared as he would never speak on a subject until over a prolonged period of time he had formed a mature judgment. His ideas were also widely disseminated through the popular religious press of the day, especially in the *Independent* and the *Christian Union*, both of which he edited for a time. Through the spoken or written word his moral earnestness shone forth and for thousands of middle-class Americans, Beecher epitomized the Christian understanding of the American experience.

Beecher was not alone in attracting great congregations. There was Phillips Brooks (1835-1893) at Trinity Episcopal Church in Boston. His pulpit style was not so noteworthy, certainly not in comparison with his saintly personality. He described preaching as "truth through personality" and in a straightforward, though poetic, rapid delivery uplifted the crowds that jammed the church for nearly a quarter of a century to hear him expound that the whole of mankind was the family of God, and that the goodness and nobility of men as children of God was the central article of his faith. A favorite phrase was "whoever has in him the human quality, whoever has the spirit of man, has the candle of the Lord." This optimism permitted him to overlook the urban conditions of the day, and to express with his middle-class parishioners the conviction that the American scene was moving toward the eventual betterment of all. Articulating a different perspective was T. DeWitt Talmage (1832-1902) at Central Presbyterian Church, Brooklyn, where with a florid style that matched his flair for sensationalism, he preached an old-fashioned religion of salvation for the sinner that was unaffected by modern currents of thought or the social implications of the Gospel but which pleased his vast congregations of rising middle-class Americans who liked to hear about the blessedness of "Mother, Home, and Heaven."

While these great preachers and many lesser ones dominated the Protestant services of worship, the church buildings themselves came to have a dominant position in the community. As mainline urban Protestant congregations grew in size so did the pretentiousness of their houses of worship. Majestic edifices of brick or stone began to rise in America's cities. These buildings testified to the affluence of the congregations and the interiors were so appointed as to continue this impression. Robed choirs began to appear, ofttimes assisted by professional singers, to lead the congregation in an increasingly formal service that was accompanied by the overpowering chords of great organs. Worship was becoming an aesthetic experience furthered by the titillating reaction to the oratory of the preacher. The eleven o'clock hour on Sunday morning was when middle-class America could celebrate the presence of God in its midst.

This new theology was not limited to these oratorical popularizers who sought to slowly lead their large congregations away from their traditional habits of thinking. There were also those devoted articulators of the faith that sought unhesitatingly to present the essence of the faith in terms of contemporary meaning. Most of these were to be found in certain theological schools, particularly those that had secured sufficient independent funding so that they were no longer under conservative and traditional denominational control. Among the denominations those that were most conducive to theological liberalism were in the urban Northeast where Congregationalism proved to be quite amenable. Also the Methodist Church in the North became permeated with these new trends, with significant inroads being made among the Episcopalians, and also to a lesser extent among the Northern Presbyterians, Baptists and the Disciples of Christ, though these latter denominations were seriously divided on the issue as witnessed by the heresy trials and the Modernist-Fundamentalist controversy that erupted after World War I.

No single individual characterizes or dominates the liberal theological tendency from the 1880's until the 1920's, but the impact on a denomination is seen in the shift from Congregationalism's Burial Hill Declaration of 1865, a basically traditional document, to the Kansas City Declaration of 1913, a predominately liberal statement.

This liberalism, called by a variety of names such as New Theology, Progressive Orthodoxy, liberal Christianity, etc., was a structured movement that espoused a rather definite doctrinal content. Reverting back to the much older theological traditions of Pelagianism or Arminianism, this theological trend emphasized the human initiative in salvation or the ability of a person to respond freely to the love of God. Building on a positive affirmation of man's capacity as well as desire for the good, sin was viewed as error and limitation which by the example of Jesus being appropriated in the individual conscience could be largely overcome. The classical doctrine of original sin or human depravity was almost entirely eliminated in such theological thinking; instead there was a great "reverence for personality" for it did indeed contain the image of God.

These theologians denied that this was a seemingly humanistic approach to religion and insisted that they were clinging tenaciously to the ancient Christocentric theological stance. William A. Brown stated it this way: "It is the method which arrives at God through Jesus, and uses the knowledge so gained as the final principle for the interpretation of life." Expanding on this is his comment: "we mean ... to trace in the ever-expanding revelation of God in humanity the vitalizing and transforming influence of the historic Jesus, that from our study we may gain new insight into the character and purpose of God from whom he came, and so be able better to understand the meaning of the world in which we live and the end to which we are called." Underlying this concept of Jesus is that he was the truly unique Son of God, not simply the man from Nazareth, but how to handle the historical problems to precisely define this was forever eluding these theologians. In defining the work of Christ, the thought expressed was more in accord with the "moral theory of the atonement" than with the historically dominant "substitutionary theory". Instead of accenting that Jesus did for man what he could not do for himself as the chief means of understanding the redemptive significance of his life and death, the emphasis was placed upon the effect the life and death of Jesus has upon the human spirit when it becomes conscious of what a life is that is totally dedicated to concretely expressing the love of God by which it is motivated.

Christ thus became the guide for the individual and the

window through which God is viewed. As such God came to be seen as "Christlike" with the emphasis being placed upon his paternalism rather than the traditional sovereignty that had long been associated with the Deity, especially in the Calvinist tradition of the Protestant faith. Along with the paternalistic emphasis went a belief in the immanence of God, an idea that was significantly buttressed by the scientific teaching of evolution as the continual unfolding of life. This could even be defined as personalism by which was accented God as "the immanent spirit of the world organism."

This theological tendency then concluded in a belief in the kingdom of God, by which was meant that this is the best category by which to express the Christian pattern of a truly redeemed community of people who were living the life as taught and practiced by Jesus, and that this was indeed the goal toward which human history was moving. The kingdom is thus already a partial social reality and is being progressively actualized and is the goal of the human story, and not just a way of describing heaven.

Many of the professors developing this theological accent received at least part of their education in Germany where they came under the influence of Hegel, Schleiermacher, Ritschl and their successors, wherein theologizing was not so dependent on the complicated processes of biblical criticism, but accented the immanence of God working out His will in history or made a direct appeal to religious experience as the means of revelation. It was not only in Europe that such thought was developing, for many of these concepts were involved in the thinking of the New England theologian, Horace Bushnell, whose seminal work, *Christian Nurture,* published in 1847, provided a native American foundation for their work.

Placing the Sermon on the Mount at the core of the Biblical message, and re-interpreting traditional dogma and the sacraments, ethical imperatives came to dominate the religious thinking of these American theologians. Also in developing systematic theological expressions and building these not on the principles of a rationalizing of the Scriptures, but upon the amplifications of religious experience, these men sought to present to the American Protestant a living faith that was contemporary with Jesus and at the same time contemporary with the post-Civil War American scene.

A small group of "scientific modernists" arose in the early years of the twentieth century, who thought that the attempt to go "back to Jesus" in the scientific world of the present was a lost cause. Thus they sought to articulate a religious faith that granted to the data of religious experience the same scientific status as the data of the physical sciences, and then to fashion a religious faith out of the materials furnished by the several sciences. Seeking a less distinctively Christian witness, these thinkers did not seek a complete break with the Christian past, but understood their approach as in the words of Shailer Mathews, "the use of the methods of modern science to find, state, and use the permanent and central values of inherited orthodoxy in meeting the needs of the modern world." Approaching religion as a human phenomenon, the Bible became one profound religious scripture among others, and Christianity one of the major religio-ethical traditions among others. This understanding of religious liberalism was not to be fully elaborated until after World War I, primarily at the University of Chicago.

Another of the religious currents to sweep over the United States in the last quarter of the nineteenth century is a movement denominated: New Thought. Clinging to familiar religious words, but investing them with quite new meanings, the articulators of New Thought placed at the central position of authority in their religion ideas that were no longer related directly to the traditional understandings of Christianity, but were related instead to modern ideas that were coming into vogue in new scientific, historical and philosophical currents of thought. New Thought had no desire to take away the positive benefits that people had acquired through their religious organizations. Using the Biblical analogy, it was asserted that New Thought had not come to destroy, but rather to fulfill—to make manifest, so far as possible, the perfect Law of God.

A major expression of this development is that which centered around "mental healing." The early American exponent of this point of view was Phineas P. Quimby of Portland, Maine, who became convinced that disease could be cured by cultivating healthy attitudes. Sickness, he declared, was the consequence of wrong beliefs and was to be overcome by the realization of healing truth. One of those who came to him for help in overcoming almost chronic illness was Mary Baker (1821-1910), better known after her third marriage as Mary Baker Eddy. She was aided by Quimby, but insisted that her own experience in 1866 led her to the realization of the answer to her physical problems. In that year she fell on the ice, and whereas her physician told her that she would not walk again, it was only three days later, upon reading Matthew 9:2 that she immediately got out of bed and was able to move easily about as if she had had no accident. To Mrs. Eddy this was the discovery of Christian Science; and she devoted the rest of her life to the development and refined articulation of what it means and the organization of an institution to strictly perpetuate these teachings. She accomplished the former in 1875 with the publication of the first of many editions of her basic textbook *Science and Health with Key to the Scriptures;* and she succeeded in the latter when in 1892 complete control of the movement was vested in the self-perpetuating Board of Trustees of the "Mother Church" in Boston and expressed three years later in *The Manual of the Mother Church.* This was the only church in the denomination as all other groups are identified as "branches" presided over by "readers" who in serving three year terms do not preach but rather read assigned passages from the Bible and the textbook, thus rigidly ensuring no deviation from the authorized teachings.

She stated her belief in the opening paragraphs of the first edition of *Science and Health:* "The control mind holds over matter becomes no longer a question when with mathematical certainty we gain its proof, and can demonstrate the facts assumed. This proof we claim to have gained, and reduced to its statement in science that furnishes a key to the harmony of man, and reveals what destroys sickness, sin, and death." Succinctly stated in *Science and Health*, the teaching is: "There is no life, truth, intelligence, no substance in matter. All is infinite Mind and its infinite manifestation, for God is All-in-all. Spirit is immortal Truth; matter is mortal error. Spirit is the real and eternal; matter is the unreal and temporal. Spirit is God, and man is His image and likeness. Therefore man is not material; he is spiritual." When one becomes aware of this, the material world, including all illnesses, is seen as an aberration of the mind and therefore as incorrect thought leading to physical conditions which have no reality in themselves. Since many of those who initially became interested in Christian Science did so for the cure of physical illness, it must be noted that real healing is conceived in terms of a spiritual breakthrough that takes place in the person's consciousness as he becomes aware of the spiritual truth so that the physical healing which then follows is only the outward manifestation of this change in consciousness. As she states in her autobiography: "Christian Science reveals God and His idea as the All and Only. It declares that evil is the absence of good; whereas, Good is God ever-present, and therefore evil is unreal and good is all that is real."

Since the denomination has always officially prohibited the publication of statistics of membership it is impossible to arrive at even an approximate size of its following; but the ideas expressed did find a large following in urban America, particularly among the more affluent female population. While not primarily a philosophy or a theology, it is a "science of health," and is promoted not only by the worship services, but by a continuous effort to explain the phenomenon of healing in the work of Christian Science Practitioners who are specifically trained to aid the members of the denomination. Also significant are the authorized lectureships that seek to present the teachings to the public and the ubiquitous presence of Christian Science reading rooms across the nation. Also identifying the movement is the highly acclaimed daily newspaper, "The Christian Science Monitor," established by Mrs. Eddy in 1908.

There have been several religious groups that have followed Mrs. Eddy, but are outside the Christian Science Church, and in so doing have modified the thrust of her teaching. One of the foremost to arise in the later part of the century was the Unity School of Practical Christianity, founded in Kansas City, Missouri, in 1889. Under its leaders, Charles and Myrtle Fillmore, it modified Mrs. Eddy's teachings by not denying the material world, but accents that through the medium of prayer we come into harmony with God and this releases the divine energies that give "abundant life and health to all God's people." The term "unity" thus sums up the principle thrust of the idea: "It embodies the central principle of what we believe: unity of the soul with God, unity of all life, unity of all religions, unity of the spirit, soul, and body: unity of all men in the heart of truth." Emphasis was initially placed on publishing and developing a corresponding clientele wherein not only the writings of the founders were sold, but specific answers to particular questions were also readily available. Eventually a more typical denominational form also came into existence.

In 1914 another facet of this movement became known as the International New Thought Alliance, and two years later stated its purpose: "to teach the infinitude of the Supreme One, the Divinity of Man and his infinite possibilities through the creative power of constructive thinking and obedience to the voice of the Indwelling Presence which is our Source of Inspiration, Power, Health and Prosperity." This thrust was not limited to just New Thought groups, but came to be expressed by many mainline Protestant clergy so that New Thought accents came to be seen by millions of Americans as central in the Protestant faith.

Other distinctly American religious developments also prospered or emerged during this same era. The followers of Joseph Smith, Jr. had been largely held together after the death of the Mormon prophet by Brigham Young, who as an astute colonizer had furthered Smith's dream by leading the Saints to the valley of the Great Salt Lake. Here in basic isolation for some time the Church of Jesus Christ of Latter-day Saints had been able to develop its theology and authoritative structure of social and economic life. With the key to its teachings summed up in the phrase: "As God once was, man now is; as God now is, man will someday become," which sounds somewhat like the statement of Protestant liberal Lyman Abbott: "What Jesus was, humanity is becoming," this optimistic group with a challenging hope developed a religious community that was to endure and become a significant factor not only in the religious life, but in the development of the Intermountain and Far West. Because of its polygamous teaching being seen as unchristian by the Protestant majority in the nation, the territory of Utah was not permitted to enter the union as a state until 1896, some six years after the Mormon president, Wilford Woodruff, had issued a proclamation declaring his intention to submit to the Supreme Court's upholding of the Congressional law forbidding plural marriages. Nonetheless, with its teachings that man, like God, is ever perfecting and moving on to greater worlds, combined with its missionary fervor, Mormonism was able to capture the affiliation of many in expressing their hopes and ideals of economic as well as spiritual advancement.

Another distinctly American religious group to make an impression on the religious scene was the movement known after 1931 as the Jehovah's Witnesses. This was a major expression of the rebirth of premillennialism that occurred after the Civil War. Founded by Charles Taze Russell in Pittsburgh in 1872, the movement taught that the second coming of Christ, in invisible form, would take place in 1874 and that the end of the present order would be in 1914. Preaching this message, later popularized by the phrase: "Millions now living will never die," Russell made successful tours of the country by appealing to the poorer classes who greatly appreciated the message that a new order was to break in and to be one in which they would materially benefit. In 1879 he began the publishing of a magazine entitled: "Zion's Watch Tower and Herald of Christ's Presence," and formally organized Zion's Watch Tower Society (not a church) in 1874. Moving to Brooklyn in 1909 he instituted the practice of publishing immense quantities of pamphlets and Bible lessons which the members of the society, called "publishers," distributed, eventually becoming known for their presence on street corners and in door to door campaigns. After his death in 1916 the leadership passed to "Judge" J.R. Rutherford, who had to deal with the fact that Jesus did not physically return to earth in 1914. The outcome was a teaching that Jesus did return at that time to reign as king in the midst of his enemies, but that this could for the time being only be understood in a spiritual sense. Rutherford further articulated that one could not date specifically the time of the physical return, but that it was imminent and would be seen in the battle of Armageddon and the destruction of evil. Asserting that God is going to bring His theocratic rule on earth, and Jesus, the perfect man, is going to establish it, the Witnesses proclaimed that the righteous would survive the battle and would enjoy this kingdom. Then would come the resurrection of the dead and a thousand-year reign of peace, after which Satan and the wicked would be destroyed. Like the Mormons, the Witnesses were not accepted by the mainline Protestants as fellow Christians, or by the political community as good Americans, the latter because of their refusal to salute the flag, register for the draft, or permit their children to receive blood transfusions, insisting that they owed allegiance only to the kingdom of God and His laws.

A far larger movement to affect the poorer element of the American populace was the Holiness Revival that erupted in Methodism, and which by the time of World War I had led to the formation of two distinctive types of denominations. This revival can be traced to the Methodist American Centenary observances in 1866 and the National Camp Meeting Association for the Promotion of Holiness organized a year later. This movement was so large that it soon appeared in nondenominational Holiness associations such as the First General Holiness Assembly which met in Chicago in 1885 and also in the formation of independent congregational forms as secessions and expulsions from the Methodist churches developed in the mid-1890's. This occurred as the Methodists became more affluent and under greater and greater influence of liberal theology and the social gospel. On the more moderate side this led to the combining of three Holiness bodies in 1908 to form the Church of the Nazarene. This new denomination, though fundamentalist in theology, was more concerned with the personal experience of Christianity and can be said to more adequately represent the perfectionism of Wesley than did the Methodist churches at that time. It became a church of simple, but yet dedicated people who wished to carry the gospel and a strict perfectionist code of morals to a large strata of Americans that the mainline denominations were not reaching, particularly in the South and Midwest.

Into the Holiness movement came another emphasis, that of the "latter rain" spoken of by the prophet Joel (2:21-32). This came to a point in the outpouring of the Spirit at the Azusa Street Mission in Los Angeles in 1906, which became a radiating point for the spread of Pentecostalism across the land, especially as consolidated in the South by A. J. Tomlinson. Being concerned not only with speaking in tongues, but also in divine healing, this movement also retained the Holiness emphasis on fundamental theology and a strict moral code, and came to be institutionally expressed in a number of churches, with the numerous Church of God organizations and the Assembly of God being the most prominent. The co-ordination of some Pentecostal activities originated in the conference held in Hot Springs, Arkansas, in 1914, and was to be followed by other associations after World War I.

The one major mainline Protestant denomination not to be affected by the theological tendencies of post-Civil War America was the Lutheran Church, organized into a sizeable number of independent national synods prior to World War I. Like the Roman Catholic Church, the German and Scandi-navian Lutherans had the task of preserving the faith in an alien land and of seeking to keep the immigrant within the fold and during this era, seeking to do so in an increasingly confessional way. Between 1870 and 1910 Lutheran church membership in the United States rose from nearly 500,000 to almost 2,500,000, almost all of it in rural and small town America, thus enabling the Lutherans to become the third largest body of Protestants in America (after the Baptists and Methodists). While the synodical structures erected in the colonial and early nineteenth century eras continued to grow, the marked Americanizing of some of these was redirected after the major flow of mid-and late-nineteenth century immigration set in, and particularly as the new synodical organizations which came into being adopted strong confessional foundations. Noted among these were the German synodical organizations centered around Buffa-lo, New York, and in Iowa, Texas, Wisconsin, and particu-larly the creation of the "German Evangelical Lutheran Synod of Missouri, Ohio, and Other States" in 1847. Under the dynamic leadership of Carl F. W. Walther, this synod enunciated an intense confessional loyalty to the sixteenth century confessions as interpreted by the seventeenth century systematic theologians. Accenting piety as well as confes-sionalism, Walther insisted that the faith was not only to be learned in the catechism, but was also the personal knowledge of the believer. His most widely read book that underscored his Lutheran theological sharpness was entitled: *The Proper Distinction Between Law and Gospel*, wherein he was also determined that Lutherans did not turn the faith into a new legalism or simple morality. Often engaged in theological debate with other Lutherans, the synod became isolated from even the rest of American Lutheranism, but held before all a determined effort to maintain its sense of confessional integrity, which was abetted by the most extensive parochial school system of any Protestant denomination in America.

The immigrants of Scandinavian origin were also of at least a nominal Lutheran background, and were quick to organize congregations in their clusters of settlement, particularly in the upper Midwest. These congregations then affiliated with synodical bodies, which were organized along the lines of national origin. While the Swedish Lutherans organized only one Lutheran church body, the Norwegians eventually created nearly a dozen synodical organizations as the attempts were made to include as many of the immigrants in a church organization that would satisfy their peculiar emphasis in the common faith. Though the story of Lutheran expansion takes on the colors of a highly complex institutional development, it does present a common conviction that the confessional faith permeated with a pietistic fervor that was brought with them was to be preserved in this land of religious freedom where all the divergencies could take on legitimate organized structures. This drive to preserve the faith of the European forefathers even affected the older Lutheran bodies in the East. But by 1917 the national identifications and pecularities within national groups had sufficiently subsisted so that the four hundreth anniversary of Martin Luther's nailing of the Ninety-five Thesis to the Castle Church door in Saxon Wittenberg could be celebrated by major mergers of Lutheran bodies, involving the uniting of most Lutherans of Norwegian extraction into a single national synod and the gathering a year later of a large number of non-Missourian German Lutherans into a single united church; and also with the creation of the National Lutheran Council a vehicle came into being whereby all Lutherans, except for the Missouri Synod and their closely aligned affiliates that had formed the Synodical Conference in 1872, could meet for increased fellowship and collective endeavor. Still the Lutherans remained largely immune from the theological currents affecting much of the rest of American Protestantism. This was due not only to the tenacious confessionalism, but also to the language question, as it was often with great reluctance, if indeed it was done at all by 1917, that the language of the church was gradually shifted to English. Though many in the younger generations clamored for the language of the public schools, many of the older generations, who had learned their Bible and catechism in the language of their national origin, just could not appreciate a secular language in matters of the sacred. It was not until long after World War I that Lutheranism was to take a creative role on the American Protestant scene, but when it did so, it could speak from the basis of a strong tradition in the faith.

Thus the complexity of the American Protestant theological scene was obvious, but this in no way deterred the denominations from attacking the missionary challenges of post-Civil War America.

2

The Industrial Challenge

The way of life in the United States changed dramatically between 1860 and 1900. The census in 1860 reported over six million "gainful workers" in agriculture, and fewer than two million in manufacturing and construction; in fact, only four million were in all nonfarming occupations combined. Twenty years later, the farmers totaled somewhat less than the eight and three-quarter million nonfarm workers, and by 1900, eighteen million nonfarm workers far outnumbered the eleven million farmers. The industrialization of America had definitely set in.

This was possible in large part to the mechanical marvels that occurred, drawing country lads and lasses to the new industrial centers, which were further burgeoned with the high influx of European immigrants. This shift was predicated on a social and political system which did give a maximum of equality, mobility and opportunity to all men; but by 1900 in the highly complex industrial order that had developed it was increasingly difficult to maintain these virtues, and many were beginning to seriously call for a reexamination of American ideals to better accomodate the American dream to the present reality.

The ability of America to produce machine-made goods and to distribute them increased prodigiously. From 1860 to 1890, the value of manufactured goods jumped from less than two billion to more than nine billion dollars. At the basis of this phenomenal growth lay the developments in rails, steel, petroleum products, processed foods, fuels, metals and communications.

The railroads led the way with the first transcontinental line being completed in 1869. Soon several such lines had been laid, and with the extensive additions of track laid east of the Mississippi River, national mileage between 1865 and 1900 increased from some 35,000 to nearly 260,000 miles. In addition to the geographical extension, such factors as common gauges, air brakes and automatic couplers had been installed, locomotives were improved, and Pullman sleeping and dining cars were added so that rail travel was comfortable for the rider, and safe and efficient for the distribution of manufactured goods.

The mass production of steel was another indicator of economic growth after the Civil War. With the introduction and development of the Bessemer process, combined with the availability of the railroads, the vast iron ore deposits around Lake Superior and the coal fields of Pennsylvania, Pittsburgh, with its roaring blast furnaces, became a glowing symbol of American economic success. It was here that Andrew Carnegie rose to financial heights, but he is also to be remembered as one of the most articulate expressors of a theology to support this accomplishment.

The development of the petroleum industry was another example of American entreprenural ability to produce enormous wealth quickly. In 1859 oil was discovered in the northwest corner of Pennsylvania at the same time a practical method for distilling raw petroleum into kerosene lamps was perfected. This potential industry came to the attention of young John D. Rockefeller, who, within twenty years, came to be the champion of the oil industry, which seemed to have unlimited possibilities with the coming of the internal combustion engine.

A Scottish traveler in Chicago in 1868 observed that in

visiting a modern slaughter house it took only twelve minutes from the time the pig was on the gangway until the pork
was packed in barrels and ready for shipment. Then with the
successful use of refrigerator cars beginning in 1875, what
had been a local business now became a national enterprise
under the direction of a few wealthy packers. In 1870 the dollar value of meat packed country-wide amounted to under
sixty-five million, but twenty years later totalled over a half
billion dollars.

The telephone had been invented by Alexander Graham
Bell in 1876, and by 1900 there were 1,356,000 across the
country, truly ushering in the Age of Unlimited Chatter.
Thomas Edison brought forth the electric light in 1879, which
soon turned the darkness into day. It is true that these great
industries produced millions of dollars for a small group of
tycoons or corporations; but it was the dream of many
young men to achieve great wealth in a bold new adventure.
Such was expressed by Mark Twain and Charles Warner in
their 1873 novel, *The Gilded Age: A Tale of Today*, when
they described the character of Philip Sterling: "He was born
into a time when all young men of his age caught the fever of
speculation, and expected to get on in the world by the omis-
sion of some of the regular processes which have been appointed from of old. And examples were not wanting to encourage him. He saw people, all around him, poor yesterday,
rich to-day, who had come into sudden opulence by some
means which they could not have classified among any of the
regular occupations of life."

The life of Andrew Carnegie (1835-1919) is a rather typical
Horatio Alger rags-to-riches story that was common to many
of the industrial tycoons that emerged on the post-Civil War
American industrial scene. Born in Scotland to a well-to-do
master weaver, the boy witnessed the erosion of the family's
financial situation as the factory system drove the hand-loom
weavers out of business. To salvage the situation for the children, Andrew's parents immigrated to Allegheny City, Penn-

sylvania, where relatives were already living. Andrew served as a "bobbin-boy" in a local cotton factory earning one dollar and twenty cents a week before his twelfth birthday. Within a year he had moved to a bobbin factory where he served in several capacities, and by the time he was fourteen had obtained a position as a messenger boy in the Pittsburgh telegraph office. Taking the initiative to learn to operate the telegraph by going to the office early in the morning before the operator arrived, he developed his technique to such an extent that when the Pennsylvania Railroad arrived in Pittsburgh and opened its own wire service, young Carnegie, because of a prior acquaintanceship with the superintendent of the railroad, was appointed his clerk and telegraph operator. Now earning thirty-five dollars a month Carnegie was not to be stopped. For thirteen years he remained in the service of the railroad, and was at the end of that time the superintendent of the Pittsburgh division. During this time his predecessor invited him to invest five hundred dollars, which Andrew managed to put together by mortgaging the family home, in the Adams Express Company. This introduced Carnegie to monthly dividends and his first experience of money earning money without physical labor on his part. He was now a businessman, in fact, a capitalist. Soon came investments in the Woodruff sleeping car, eventually bought out by George Pullman, and then in the Keystone Bridge Works, which introduced him to the iron industry. Resigning from the Pennsylvania, Carnegie in 1865 entered into his life's work with iron and steel. While not introducing, but developing the Bessemer process in the manufacture of steel, and gaining control over enormous coal and iron-ore properties, he built mills to manufacture finished steel products so that by the nineties he was the most advanced and the most powerful industrialist in the American steel and iron industry. In 1901 he sold out to the financiers organized by the nation's most powerful banker, J. P. Morgan, for a reputed price of $492,000,000.

Writing in the *North American Review* in 1889, Carnegie confessed: "The problem of our age is the proper administration of wealth." He sincerely felt that there was a proper distribution of wealth under the economic system of laissez-faire capitalism that would ensure "that the ties of brotherhood may still bind together the rich and poor in harmonious relationship." While he admitted that the price which society pays for the law of competition so inherent in the capitalistic system is great, and indeed may be overbearingly hard for the individual in many instances, it is best for the race. This is true not only because it insures the survival of the fittest in every department of life; but it is also due to this law that we owe our wonderful material development, which it must be remembered betters the lives of all individuals when the contemporary way of life is compared with that of even a short time before. This led him to encapsulate his defense of the capitalistic system by saying: "We accept and welcome, therefore, as conditions to which we must accommodate ourselves, great inequality of environment; the concentration of business, industrial and commercial in the hands of a few; and the law of competition between these, as being not only beneficial, but essential to the future progress of the race."

In discussing the person who has the ability to conduct affairs upon a great scale he insists that considerable latitude be given them, for "it is a law...that men possessed of this peculiar talent for affairs, under the free play of economic forces must, of necessity, soon be in receipt of more revenue than can be judiciously expended upon themselves." Though he does not explicitly state that such gifted men are the elect of God, the inference appears not to be far below the surface. This may be seen in his later reference to the parable of the talents recorded in Matthew 25:14-28 where to those who had accumulated and even doubled their capital, the Lord said: "Well done, thou good and faithful servant; thou has been faithful over a few things, I will make thee ruler over many things; enter thou into the joy of the Lord." Stating such a position unequivocally was Bishop William Lawrence of the Massachusetts Episcopal Diocese when he uttered: "Godliness is in league with riches", so that "in the long run, it is only to the man of morality that wealth comes." Stating the obverse was Henry Ward Beecher: "the general truth will stand, that no man in this land suffers from poverty unless it be more than his fault—unless it be his sin." As wealth was an individual accomplishment, so too poverty was not seen as a corporate reality, but was also individual, and in this case, the mark of individual failure, whether or not this was described as sin.

Continuing the development of his thought, Carnegie writes that "upon the sacredness of property civilization itself depends." At this point he is not hesitant to use the language of religion. Having successfully argued, at least to his own satisfaction, that the laws upon which civilization is founded have thrown the wealth into the hands of the few, he offers what he believes is the true solution to its distribution.

He elaborates on the three modes by which surplus wealth can be distributed. "It can be left to the families of the descendents; or it can be bequeathed for public purposes; or, finally it can be administered by its possessors during their lives." The first two alternatives he finds unsatisfactory; the first because the heirs will likely squander it in unproductive lives and not make the assets of the estate available to the improvement of civilization. The second alternative is injudicious in that it implies that the testor would not have left it at all if he had been able to take it with him; and anyway it is the responsibility of the accumulator to distribute it as he is more fit to do so than some public agency. At this point he injects a defense of not paying higher wages as a means of judiciously administering wealth. His point is that the masses do not know how to manage money and that it will become "wasted in the indulgence of appetite, some of it in excess, and it may be doubted whether even the part put to the best use, that of adding to the comforts of the homes, would have yielded results for the race comparable to what a wise administrator is able to do." There were many who would quickly add the rejoinder that the salaries being paid the factory workers were not even sufficient to maintain a minimal living standard so that even necessary comforts could not be added; but they would also have to agree with Carnegie that too often certain appetites were indulged in to excess.

The theology, as it were, that Carnegie was expressing is summed up in this paragraph:

> This, then, is held to be the duty of the man of wealth; To set an example of modest, unostentatious living, shunning display or extravagance; to provide moderately for the legitimate wants of those dependent upon him; and, after doing so, to consider all surplus revenues which come to him simply as trust funds, which he is called upon to administer, and strictly bound as a matter of duty to administer in the manner which, in his judgment, is best calculated to produce the most beneficial results for the community—the man of wealth thus becoming the mere trustee and agent for his poorer brethren, bringing to their service his superior wisdom, experience, and ability to administer, doing for them better than they would or could do for themselves.

Later he came across a sermon preached by the Rev. John Wesley, founder of the society called Methodist in the midst of the industrial revolution in later eighteenth century England; and found in this a passage that encapsulated his thought. Carnegie stated: "Upon this sermon the gospel of wealth seems founded. Indeed, had I known of its existence before writing upon the subject, I should certainly have quoted it." The statement as he later used it reads:

> Gain all you can by honest industry. Use all possible diligence in your calling. Lose no time. Gain all you can by common sense, by using in your business all the understanding which God has given you. It is amazing to observe how few do this—how men run on in the same dull track with their forefathers.

Having gained all you can by honest wisdom and un-wearied diligence, the second rule of Christian prudence is, "Save all you can." Do not throw it away in idle expenses—to gratify pride, etc. If you desire to be a good and faithful steward, out of that portion of your Lord's goods which he has for the present lodged in your hands, first provide things needful for yourself, food, raiment, etc.

Second provide these for your wife, your children, your servants, and others who pertain to your household. If then you have an overplus do good to them that are of the household of faith. If there be still an overplus, do good to all men.

In outlining means of distribution, Carnegie was careful to allow each man of wealth the prerogative of determining how in his situation the money under his trusteeship could be dispensed to bring the greatest good. He did warn against, however, the common practice of charity as traditionally understood. He was unalterably opposed to indiscriminate charity; he declaimed "it was better for mankind that the millions of the rich were thrown into the sea than so spent as to encourage the slothful, the drunken, the unworthy." The statistic he used to support this contention is that "of every thousand dollars spent in so-called charity today, it is probable that nine hundred fifty dollars is unwisely spent, indeed, as to produce the very evils which it hopes to mitigate or cure." Beggars, he insists, were only encouraged by being the recipients of charity and never seek to rise out of their condition so long as they can make their way by this means. In a subsequent essay entitled "The Advantages of Poverty" he asserted that "every drunken vagabond or lax idler supported by alms bestowed by wealthy people is a source of moral infection to a neighborhood," a point of view also shared by the reformer, Jacob Riis, in his 1890 study of the New York tenements. Carnegie's position was that "in bestowing charity, the main consideration should be to help those who will help themselves; to provide part of the means by which those who desire to improve may do so; to give those who desire to rise the aids by which they may rise, to assist, but rarely or never to do all."

In a second article also published in 1889 in the *North American Review*, Carnegie went on to discuss the best fields of philanthropy for the persons whose income was more than mere compensation for their own immediate needs. The first category he enunciated was the founding of a university. Though he could point to some examples of this, and there would be several more in ensuing decades, he thought there was a limit to the number of new schools needed; but there would always be a need for additions to existing institutions, and to this cause he directed the thoughts of the very rich, and also the not so wealthy. His second suggestion was the one most dear to his own heart, that of the gift of a free library to a community; provided, of course, as was true of all distributions of these so-called trustee funds, that the community will accept and maintain the gift as a public institution, as much a part of the city property as its public schools, and in the specific case of the library, an adjunct to these. Stating why his personal preference was for libraries, he recalled his own boyhood and the fond memories he had of a Colonel Anderson, who every Saturday made his personal library of four hundred volumes available to the boys of the neighborhood. Carnegie states that while he was a youth enjoying these books he resolved that if wealth ever came to him it should be used to establish free libraries that "other poor boys might receive opportunities similar to those for which he was indebted to that noble man." Closely allied to the library, and where possible to be a part of it there should be rooms for an art gallery, museum and a hall for lectures. What he is urging here is that the practices of many European cities be copied since there were so few cultural institutions in this country in comparison to what was available in even the smaller European cities.

Another area of possibility for the trustee was the founding and, more likely, extension of hospitals, medical colleges,
laboratories, and other institutions connected with the allevi-
ation of human suffering, and especially with the prevention
rather than with the cure of human ills. Moving from the care
of the body physically to a more aesthetic development of the
human spirit is the creation of public parks or their improvement, provided of course, that such undertakings become the
permanent responsibility of the community for maintenance.
Another cultural area is the providing by the benefactor of
halls suitable for meetings of all kinds, and for concerts of
elevating music, most certainly including a fine organ. A
final form of benevolence, which is again common in Europe,
is the establishment of "swimming baths" for the use of all
people.

As a footnote he did also include the category of churches
as fields for the use of surplus wealth, but because of their
sectarian nature in the United States these institutions do not
generally benefit all of society, but only a selected group.
Nonetheless there are occasions when a struggling church is
truly seeking to serve an entire neighborhood and is able to
give evidence of making considerable progress in doing so.
Such a church is worthy of support to enable it to more effectively serve as the center of social life and source of neighbor-
ly feeling.

In summing up his "gospel" he states: "The only point required by the gospel of wealth is that the surplus which
accrues from time to time in the hands of a man should be
administered by him in his own lifetime for that purpose
which is seen by him, as trustee, to be best for the good of the
people." This to Carnegie is the literal obedience to the
admonition of Christ that had for centuries been so important to the monastic ideal, but is now being correctly understood in capitalistic post-Civil War industrial America; that
admonition being the advice Christ gave to the rich young
ruler who asked him how to be saved, and which upon real-

izing that he loved his money told him: "Sell all that you have, give to the poor, and come , follow me." To one who practiced this by distributing his extra wealth judiciously Carnegie said the scriptural statement: "It is easier for a camel to enter the eye of a needle than for a rich man to enter the kingdom of heaven" did not apply for to the trustee of great riches, such riches are no bar at the gates of Paradise.

In the midst of the "Robber Barons" stood Andrew Carnegie, individualist to the core, but yet also sensitive to the entire human scene; who could proclaim that "to die rich is to die disgraced," and carried this out by expending more than $311,000,000 of funds available to him as trustee. In addition to his outlay of more than $43,000,000 in the building of 2,507 public libraries, he financed technical training at the Carnegie Institute of Technology, encouraged research in basic science by the Carnegie Institution in Washington, and aided college teachers through the establishment of a pension fund through the Carnegie Foundatio.1 for the Advancement of Teaching. Of special interest to him was the Carnegie Endowment for International Peace and of very great significance was the creation of the Carnegie Corporation of New York, which as a separate foundation was as large as all his other trusts combined having an initial endowment of $125,000,000 "to promote the advancement and diffusion of knowledge and understanding among the people of the United States." This was to be done by aiding technical schools, institutions of higher learning, libraries, scientific research and publications.

The best known popular propagandist of the gospel of wealth was the Rev. Russell Conwell (1843-1925). While Carnegie was a bit elitist in his thinking, assuming that only a few had the ability to make millions, Conwell was far more proletarian assuming that all were intended by God to become affluent. This was the thrust of his well known lecture "Acres of Diamonds" which he reputedly delivered more than six thousand times. He told his auditors in the midst of the lecture: "unless some of you get richer for what I am saying tonight my time is wasted." He would continue by asserting; "I say that you ought to get rich, and it is your duty to get rich...Because to make money honestly is to preach the gospel." Though he admitted that some of the men of wealth had gotten their fortunes by dishonest means, he was of the convinction that "ninety-eight out of one hundred of the rich men of America are honest." To Conwell "that is why they are rich. That is why they are trusted with money. That is why they carry on great enterprises and find plenty of people to work with them."

In further expounding on this theme, he underscores another basic part of the American ideology of the time by declaring: "A man is not really a man until he owns his own home, and they that own their homes are made more honorable and honest and pure, and true and economical and careful, by owning the home." This dream was not then a frequent urban reality, for in 1875 only one man in a hundred engaged in the industries of Massachusetts owned a house. From this assumption it is easy to move to the theme "Money is power, and you ought to be reasonably ambitious to have it. You ought because you can do more good with it than you could without it." Therefore "if you can honestly attain unto riches...it is your Christian and godly duty to do so." Conwell then quickly answers the query as to what about the poor, by blatantly proclaiming: "There is not a poor person in the United States who was not made poor by his own shortcomings, or by the shortcomings of someone else. It is all wrong to be poor, anyhow." Since the number of poor who are to be sympathized with is very small, the lecturer declares "to sympathize with a man whom God has punished for his sins, thus to help him when God would still continue a just punishment, is to do wrong, no doubt about it, and we do that more than we help those who are deserving." In this lecture he also allows himself to be asked whether or not there is anything of greater value than money; to which he responds: "love is the grandest thing on God's earth, but fortunate the lover who has plenty of money." Conwell was then careful to point out that the love of money is indeed sinful; that the purpose of money is to develop character and to advance the human race.

The lecturer than turns to the practical thrust of the presentation; namely, how does one make money? He warns against falling victim to the cliche: "the grass is greener on the other side of the fence." The lecture opens with the account of Conwell riding a camel along the Euphrates River in the Near East and being regaled with stories by the Arab guide. One story in particular is remembered, and that is the tale of Ali Hafed who was a wealthy farmer, that is, until a priest visited him and told him of the greater wealth to be amassed in the collection of diamonds. This made the farmer feel impoverished, and he asked where he could obtain such diamonds; and when the priest told him of the topographical features in which diamonds were usually found the farmer disposed of his holdings and went in search of the diamond fields, and after exhausting himself in a fruitless search the impoverished and disappointed man cast himself into the sea. Now it so happened that the man who bought the farm was out watering his camel when he observed a curious flash of light from the sands of the stream. Bending over he pulled out a stone having an eye of light reflecting all the hues of the rainbow. Setting this on his mantel it was later observed by that same priest who immediately identified it as a diamond. Upon further search, this farm was discovered to be in the center of a field of diamonds.

The moral of this story is then translated into late nineteenth century urban terms when Conwell advises his hearers that if they wish great wealth not to go from home, but "oh, my friends, if you will just take only four blocks around you, and find out what the people want and what you ought to supply and set them down with your pencil, and figure up the profits you would make if you did supply them, you would very soon see it. There is wealth right within the sound of your voice," and you do not need inherited wealth to get a start; in fact, most rich men's sons are failures. Instead, "you must first know the demand; you must first know what people need, and then invest yourself where you are most needed." He gives such examples as the man who tied a rubber on the end of a stick that with a very small investment led to the rubber-tipped pencil in such common use, or the man who devised the safety pin to meet another obvious need.

So it was that both businessmen and Protestant clergy could attempt to make peace with the reigning "rugged individualism" with its acquisitive urge, and the Christian concept of concern for one's fellowmen. This sense of individualism "came to mean in practice that no matter what an individual did in following his own even selfish desires or whims it would ultimately be seen as in harmony with the best interests of the whole society."[1] This gave a new impetus to the Puritan ideal of hard work and frugality in a new industrialized society, a point of view reinforced by the Methodist teaching; and at the same time gave a divine sanction to the industrialist and a religious reason for increasing the wealth of the nation. The end result was an increasing alignment of American Protestantism with the rising middle and upper classes of society in what has been described as a "culture religion" that made the entrepreneurs complacent as presumably Christian businessmen building the kingdom of God on earth.

The story of the American experience was not so neat and humanitarian as the gospel of wealth suggested. The rapid growth of American industry after the Civil War led to the creation of even greater concentrations of economic power in fewer and fewer corporations. It has been noted that by 1890 one percent of the families actually owned over half of the nation's wealth. The individual laborer was indeed becoming more and more dependent on the machine that he operated but did not own. That aspect of the spirit of the age which assumed that the material blessings being made possible would also redound to the comfort of millions of Americans was being questioned by the laborer, who also saw that in adjusting to being the employee of the giant, impersonal corporation that his integrity as a craftsman was being ignored leaving as his only marketable ability the strength of his hands to operate a machine in a dirty, noisy and sweaty factory that was also likely devoid of safety precautions. Furthermore, he had no way to even demand a living wage, for he was easily replaced by another newcomer to the city who was anxious for a job. In working for exploitative wages, and subject to seasonal as well as sudden layoffs, he sensed that alone he could not escape from this system of production, and he began to chafe as he lost his pride in his work and control over his livelihood.

Labor organizations, which already had a history in this country, hesitatingly and without a firm sense of direction, gradually sought to right the situation. By 1880 the idealistic hopes of labor union programs to purify society without conflict fell by the side. Instead new organizations appeared seeking such short-term goals as the eight-hour day, abolition of child labor, eradicaton of convict labor, controls on immigration, and the end of the company store where salaries were paid in overpriced, but inferior goods. To secure this and the increase in wages that was always a major concern, provisions were made for the further development and use of the weapons of strike and boycott. The Bureau of Labor reported that during the last two decades of the nineteenth century there were 23,798 strikes and 1005 lockouts putting a total of 6,610,000 out of work in 132,442 plants.

The Protestant churches were much slower to react to this rather swift change in American economic life. Firmly entrenched in the American version of Calvinist and Wesleyan thought inspiring one to hard work and fiscal responsibility, the American Protestant churches continued to see in the industrial rise the material blessings stemming from the faithful practice of religious convictions. As to the laborer, the common attitude was expressed by a writer in the June 4, 1874 issue of the *Watchman and Reflector*: "Labor is a commodity, and like all other commodities, its condition is governed by the imperishable laws of demand and supply. It is all right to talk and declaim about the dignity of labor...But when all has been said of it, what is labor but a matter of barter and sale?" A noted student of the American Protestant scene has summed it up this way: "In 1876 Protestantism presented a massive, almost unbroken front in its defense of the social status quo."[2]

The nation was stunned by the violent labor upheavals of 1877 when striking railroad men protested against pay cuts that would reduce their average earnings by ten percent, this on top of previous wage cuts and widespread unemployment in the wake of the depression that had struck four years earlier. A series of unrelated outbursts climaxed in Pittsburgh where strikers against the Pennsylvania Railroad were joined by a mob of supporters who raged through the streets and set fire to the Union Depot, shops, offices and hundreds of freight cars. With the Pittsburgh militia unwilling to fight the twenty thousand raging men, a Philadelphia militia unit had to be called upon to quell the outburst. Mob rule lasted four days and nearly fifty rioters and some of the soldiers were shot before order was restored.

The religious press of the day, admittedly more outspoken than the denominational assemblies, brought forth heated denunciations which saw these disturbances as indicating a struggle between anarchy and order. The press exonerated the honest workingman and denounced the foreign and communist agitators that had incited the riots. The religious editors encouraged that the grievances be settled, but did not recognize the naescent labor unions as an issue in this situation, for this was a moral rather than economic or social problem. The *Independent* made this clear when it stated on July 26, 1877: "The government cannot wisely undertake the task of regulating the relations of capital and labor beyond the simple duty of enforcing contracts." Instead solutions such as education, profit-sharing, industry and sobriety were offered as partial remedies; but the cry was raised throughout the churches that the government use whatever military force necessary to restore and maintain law and order, as seen in this statement in the *Independent* on August 2: "Whenever a riot appears, the only thing to be done is to apply to it with unsparing severity the law of force. If the club of the policemen knocking out the brains of the rioter will answer, well and good; but if not, than bullets and bayonets, canister and grape, constitute the one remedy and the one duty of the hour."

Less than ten years later in 1886 the nation witnessed another dramatic outpouring of labor unrest. Workers at the McCormick Harvester plant in Chicago struck in protest against the firing of union members, and in turn had been locked out. Later a crowd of these locked-out workers attacked strikebreakers as they were leaving the plant and when police joined the fracas several strikers were killed. A member of the anarchist International Working People's Association printed a circular that called for revenge, and a protest meeting was held the next night in Haymarket Square that amounted to nothing more than heated oratory until a police detail suddenly appeared to break up the meeting. Then a bomb was lobbed from a still unknown source and from the explosion and subsequent police firearms seven officers were killed and at least sixty people injured. A wave of hysteria swept Chicago and extended nationwide leading to a notorious trial in which eight anarchists were arrested and tried for the crime on a loose indictment containing nearly seventy counts without ever establishing any connection between the defendents and the throwing of the so-called "anarchist made" bomb. The verdict was that one received a fifteen year sentence and seven were condemned to death. Of the seven, one committed suicide, four were hanged and two had their sentences commuted.

The response of the American Protestant community to this was to react in shock and horror, but even in spite of the nationwide repulsion that occurred, there was at least in the religious press a greater understanding of the principle of labor organization and a nod of support for the Knights of Labor. Again the honest worker was absolved, and even the unions were not blamed for the rioting. However, the unions were charged with inaugurating strikes that had provided the opportunity for physical outbreaks. The principle was enunciated that strikes and boycotts were dangerous weapons that were as likely to injure the public and the workingman as much as the employers against whom the strike was directed. Though the strike and boycott were condemned by the religious press, the unions were given some legitimacy; the denominational assemblies, however, still preferred to remain silent on the labor problem or were very carefully guarded in their statements about it.

Nonetheless, with the increase in the pace of consolidation leading to the gigantic trusts with industry-wide powers of control, the people acting through Congress took initial steps in seeking answers to questions concerning economic justice and the means of hopefully reconciling a highly organized society and the free individual. Preliminary steps in this direction were the Interstate Commerce Act of 1887 and the Sherman Antitrust Act three years later.

Then near Pittsburgh in 1892 occurred the Homestead Steel strike against the giant industrialist Andrew Carnegie, who called in Pinkerton guards to disperse the rioters, but when this failed troops restored order. Then two years later came the infamous Pullman strike that received national attention when the president of the United States, over the objections of the governor of Illinois, sent in federal troops to protect the mails being carried on the trains using Pullman cars. The reactions in the religious press to these labor upheavals was very similar to that of the eighties, with an ominous note being shared that it was feared that union labor could not refrain from the resort to violence, and also from the coercion of the non-union worker. The press was now less friendly to organized labor than it had been a decade earlier.

American Protestantism continued to condemn the strikes and to tell the poor workingman to work harder, or to wait for God to change the situation; the simplistic excuse that greed at the top could be ignored or accepted as a tool of progress while misery at the bottom could be waved aside as inevitable or, at most, treated by a program of guarded and labeled philanthropy did not satisfy increasing numbers of sensitive religionists. The strikes of the era forced many in the churches to admit the existence of problems that had been ignored, and after every outbreak, and its resultant denunciation, there were attempts at constructive analysis and solution. It was indeed the catalyst of the labor agitation that forced the churches to begin reassessing the American economic scene.

Though it was easier to be critical than to offer a constructive alternative, which was often sentimental and utopian when offered, the last twenty years of the nineteenth century provided a time more for discussion than practical application of the principles of what came to be called social Christianity. The term "social Christianity" came to be used more than "applied Christianity," because, while in the 1880's the reaction of the churches was against socialism and labor rather than wealth and the cities, by the 1890's socialism had been somewhat accepted, not in its materialistic or atheistic aspects, but in its teaching concerning the solidarity of the race as opposed to individualism. Though some of the articulators of social Christianity did draw some of their beliefs from socialist ideas and programs, "in general they were progressive and reformist rather than reconstructionist or revolutionary in their thought and action."[3] Yet, the theological content that did slowly emerge made social Christianity unable to provide the great mass of Christians with the spiritual sustenance they demanded and so did not penetrate the great masses. With its doctrine of God couched in the portrayal of an ethical, imminent and human view of God rather than the Biblical prophetic God, there was not much gap between God and man; and with the accent on service to man being service to God this led to an identification of the religious and cultural values which brought God from heaven and made Him a part of the universe which can serve the ends of man. The simplicity and optimism of its social analysis did not prepare social Christianity to lead the way through the problems of the twentieth century.

Rather, when in 1902 the United Mine Workers struck the anthracite coal industry, the response of George F. Baer, the president of the Reading Railway, which controlled half of the hard-coal mines, reflected the dominant Protestant pattern of thought: "The rights and interests of the laboring man will be protected and cared for—not by the labor agitators, but by the Christian men to whom God in His infinite wisdom has given the control of the property interests of the country." Nonetheless the union, under the deft management of John Mitchell, won the sympathy of millions, including President Theodore Roosevelt, who sought to serve as an arbiter in the dispute. Eventually arbitration did for a short time conclude the strike with favorable results for the miners. However, organized labor's balance sheet up to the time of World War I was hardly a success story, as the unions had accomplished relatively little in the way of raising living standards for the millions who were poor.

Another direction had to be pursued to significantly shift the American middle-class point of view, and this came with the sudden elevation of Theodore Roosevelt to the presidency in 1901, and particularly after he was himself elected to that office in 1904. Within two months of the election Roosevelt boldly declared:

> Unquestionably...the great development of industrialism means that there must be an increase in the supervision exercised by the Government over business enter-

prises.... Neither this people nor any other free people will permanently tolerate the use of the vast power conferred by vast wealth, and especially by wealth in its corporate form, without lodging somewhere in the Government the still higher power of seeing that this power, in addition to being used in the interest of the individual or individuals possessing it, is also used for and not against the interests of the people as a whole.

Meaning specifically the federal government, Roosevelt defended the recent action of the Supreme Court in sustaining his attempt to break up J.P. Morgan's Northern Security Company as a violation of the Sherman Antitrust Act, and to point toward the successful passage of the Hepburn Act to regulate freight rates on the nation's railroads. Dismayed with his successor, William Howard Taft, in his progressive program, Roosevelt finally became the leader of a third party in the 1912 election, and blurted: "Our cause is based on the eternal principal of righteousness." The party's platform was identified by the candidate as his "Confession of Faith," and he took as his theme song "Onward Christian Soldiers." However, the election went to Woodrow Wilson, who though not enamored with the use of the power of the federal government to right the wrongs of society eventually came around to Roosevelt's position as the Clayton Act of 1915 strengthened the Sherman Act and declared that labor organizations should not be treated by the courts as conspirators in restraint of trade. More significant was the Federal Trade Commission Act, which did create a government agency with the power of overseeing and restraining practically all big business.

Though social Christianity failed to convert religious conservatives or to attract labor support, it did achieve considerable influence when it along with other forces was able to redirect the thinking of the progressive middle class.

One of the pioneers in constructive work in the realm of social Christianity was Washington Gladden (1836-1918) who wrote extensively, especially while pastor of the First Congregational Church in Columbus, Ohio, from 1882 until his death. He advocated the right of labor to organize and yet encouraged cooperation of labor and capital in an attempt to reduce the competitve nature of American industry. He also sought to encourage profit-sharing, as well as a reduction in the number of hours a man was expected to work daily. Both of these goals had long been denounced by churchmen. What Gladden was seeking was social ameliora-tion by the direct application of the ethic of love, this then leading him not to be obsessed with sin and salvation, but rather to preach the fatherhood of God and the brotherhood of man. He was successful in doing so in terms that were understandable and acceptable to the untheoretical, worldly, optimistic congregations of his time. His writings were pri-marily tracts for the times that did articulate a growing con-viction of many churchmen. He was careful not to outdis-tance his audiences, as for example addressing himself to the concept of the Fatherhood of God in 1899 he made the point that in the history of Christian theology "the paternal char-acter was wholly submerged in the kingly character. Father-hood was a vague and distant possibility; the immediate, awful, overwhelming fact was sovereignty." He went on to note how this had happened when Christianity came under the tutelage of the Roman Empire; but now in free America is the opportunity to shed this unfortunate historical accretion and return to the teachings of Jesus. The law of brotherhood which directly follows from Christ's doctrine of Fatherhood is the only solution for the problems of society. This teaching provides "but one law for home and school and shop and factory and market and court and legislative hall. One child of the common Father cannot enslave another nor exploit another; the strong and the fortunate and the wise cannot take advantage of the weak and the crippled and the ignorant, and enrich themselves by spoiling their neighbor; each must care for the welfare of all, and all must minister to the good of each." In the last decade of his life he reiterated this position by stating: "the establishment and maintenance of sound and fair social conditions, so that there should be no oppression nor injustice, but a square deal for everybody," was his goal. He asserted that this would lead to the strong not being permitted to prey on the weak, "so that the law of helpfulness should prevail, instead of the law of ravin." Such conditions would bring "unexampled and marvelous prosperity," and along with this peace and happiness. He is still remembered for his hymns expressing this theology, the most famous being "O Master, Let Me Walk with Thee."

O Master, let me walk with thee
In lowly paths of service free;
Tell me thy secret; help me bear
The strain of toil, the fret of care.

Help me the slow of heart to move
By some clear, winning word of love;
Teach me the wayward feet to stay,
And guide them in the homeward way.

Teach me thy patience; still with thee
In closer, dearer company,
In work that keeps faith sweet and strong,
In trust that triumphs over wrong.

In hope that sends a shining ray
Far down the future's broadening way,
In peace that only thou canst give;
With thee, O Master, let me live.

In 1900, Harvard Professor Francis G. Peabody published his *Jesus Christ and the Social Question*, in which he pointedly advanced the social gospel by arguing that "the social question of the present age is not a question of mitigating the evils of the existing order, but a question whether the existing order itself shall last. It is not so much a problem of social amelioration which occupies the modern mind, as a problem of social transformation and reconstruction." Thus, by the turn of the century, there was a marked divergence from the point of view in the Protestant community as compared to a score of years earlier.

The foremost leader in the development of a theology for social Christianity in America was Walter Rauschenbusch (1861-1918). Educated in Germany and at Rochester Theological Seminary, he took as his first parish the Second German Baptist Church in the proximity of the "Hell's Kitchen" area of New York City, where he served following his graduation from the seminary in 1886 until 1897. In this congregation in one of the city's notorious slums, Rauschenbusch came to realize that the individualistic piety of popular American Protestantism failed to solve the new urban problems that confronted his parishioners. He sought direction from Henry George and other social critics, and in 1892 was a cofounder of the Brotherhood of the Kingdom, which was one of the earliest groups of churchmen who wished to emphasize the social aspects of the gospel. In 1897 the opportunity to devote himself more exclusively to the study of social Christianity came when he was invited to join his father in Rochester Seminary's German school. Five years later this culminated in his being made professor of church history on the regular faculty, a position he held until his death.

Actively pursuing his interests, he became internationally known in 1907 with the publication of *Christianity and the Social Crisis*. This was not a socialist tract, but a conservative study of the history of Christianity, albeit from a social view asserting that "religion is the hallowing of all life." In examining the life of Jesus he was quick to point out that "in truth Jesus was not a social reformer of the modern type. Sociology and political economy were just as far outside of his range of thought as organic chemistry or the geography of America." Yet, Jesus saw the evil in the lives of people and was sensitive to their sufferings, but he approached these facts solely from the moral, and not from the economic or historical point of view. In so doing, Rauschenbusch insisted that Jesus reverted back "to the earlier and nobler prophetic view of the ancient Israelites that the future was to grow out of the present by divine help." He did not accept the point of view of many of his contemporaries that awaited a Messianic cataclysm that would bring the kingdom of God ready-made from heaven. Rather he took his illustrations from organic life "like the seed scattered by the peasant, growing slowly and silently, night and day, by its own germinating force and the food furnished by the earth." Rauschenbush realized that the contemporaries of Jesus, like so many of his contemporaries, were impatient and did not see processes, but clamored for results, and big thunderous, miraculous results. Rauschenbusch insisted that Jesus had the rare ability of scientific insight by which "he grasped the substance of that law of organic development in nature and history which our own day at last has begun to elaborate systematically." The Rochester professor goes on to state that though Jesus worked on individuals and through individuals "his real end was not individualistic, but social, and in his method he employed strong social forces." Realizing that a new view of life would have to be implanted before it could be lived he also sensed that the new society would have to nucleate around personal centers of renewal. Yet the ultimate goal was not the new soul, but rather the new society.

Ten years later Rauschenbusch wrote *A Theology of the Social Gospel*, as social Christianity had by now come to be known. In this he tried to rebut the charges that the social gospel was a movement in search of a theology, but had never really found one, to specifically delineate what he meant by the doctrine of the fall, and to give a definition of sin since these doctrines so central to traditional Christianity seemed to be significantly altered by Rauschenbusch and even more so by many social gospel advocates. He summed up the traditional position by stating that the doctrine of the fall has been taught to mean the regarding of evil "as a kind of unvarying racial element, which is active in every new life and which can be overcome only by the grace offered in the Gospel and ministered by the Church." He countered this position with the thrust that "evil could be regarded instead as a variable factor in the life of humanity, which it is our duty to diminish for every young life and for every new generation." The synonym that Rauschenbusch used for sin is "selfishness". "The sinful mind, then, is the unsocial and anti-social mind;" or to be more specific: "social groups who have turned the patrimony of a nation into the private property of a small class, or have left the peasant laborers cowed, degraded, demoralized, and without rights in the land." Whenever such a situation is seen "we shall know we have struck real rebellion against God on the higher levels of sin." Continuing his search for definition he writes: "A theology for the social gospel would have to say that original sin is partly social. It runs down the generations not only by biological propagations but also by social assimilation." Possibly realizing that he was not clearly articulating a position, and also wishing to place his thoughts within the orbit of traditional Christianity he stipulated that what he was saying could not be dispatched simply by saying that sin was the force of evil example. He insisted that there is much more involved: "We deal here not only with the instinct of imitation, but with the spiritual authority of society over its members." In a back-handed attack on many of his theological contemporaries he chided: "to concentrate our efforts on personal salvation, as orthodoxy has done, or on soul culture, as liberalism has done, comes close to refined selfishness." He insisted that what he was doing was making the best use of the new historical insights coming from the German theological faculties. In so doing he charged the traditional theology as being above time and history giving a static concept of salvation and its reception by having everyone at all times and in all places going "through the same process of repentance, faith, justification, and regeneration and who in due time die and go to heaven or hell." The social gospel is historically minded as it "tries to see the progress of the Kingdom of God in the flow of history; not only in the doings of the Church, but in the clash of economic forces and social classes."

In the preface to his 1907 publication he declares "that the essential purpose of Christianity was to transform human society into the kingdom of God by regenerating all human relations and reconstituting them in accordance with the will of God." A decade later he stated it in a crisp sentence: "Salvation is the voluntary socializing of the soul," or in another short sentence: "the social gospel is concerned about a progressive social incarnation of God."

Central to this presentation of Christianity was the concept of the Kingdom of God as an evolutionary development in which by working together God and man overcome the forces of evil and inaugurate the reign of justice, democracy and brotherhood on earth. While he could speak of the Kingdom of God as a collective conception which was "not a matter of getting individuals to heaven, but of transforming the life on earth into the harmony of heaven," he was also careful to state in the same book that of the two great entities in human life—the human soul and the human race—religion was to save both. "The soul is to seek righteousness and eternal life; the race is to seek righteousness and the kingdom of God."

In carefully trying to delineate wherein popular traditional pietistic Protestantism had veered too far from the biblical and early Christian roots of the faith, he deplored that Christians had become "accustomed to connect piety with the thought of private virtues; the pious man is the quiet, temperate, sober kindly man. The evils against which we contend in the churches are intemperance, unchastity, the sins of the tongue." The truth of the matter historically is that "the twin-evils against which the prophets launched the condemnation of Jehovah were injustice and oppression." Furthermore the preoccupation of modern Christianity with eternal life for the individual as the Christian hope has meant that the kingdom of God receded to the background, and with it went much of the social potency of Christianity." Concommitent with this was the common assertion that it is not the church's task to speak out on social and economic issues for such efforts before the coming of the Lord are doomed to failure; this being true because the environment has no saving power so that regeneration is what men need. It can be summed up with the assertion that we do not live for this world, but for the life to come. The popular hymns like "I'm but a stranger here, heaven is my home" summed up the popular view.

In response to this Rauschenbusch boldly proclaims that "religious individualism lacks the triumphant faith in the possible sovereignty of Jesus Christ in all human affairs, and therefore it lacks the vision and the hearld voice to see and proclaim his present conquest and enthronement." Furthermore individualistic piety "lacks that vital interest in the totality of human life which can create a united and harmonious and daring religious conception of the world." Instead of seeking to escape this world for the glory of the ivory palaces of popular hymnody and in the meantime to lead an ascetic life of confession, "the millennial hope is the social hope of Christianity."

Rauschenbush was as harsh in his judgment of the church as an institution as he was in regard to its theology. He felt that the church had once again substituted itself for the kingdom of God, and had therefore put the advancement of a tangible and very human organization in the place of the moral uplifting of humanity. In making its own organization the chief object of social service, it magnified what the individual did for the church and belittled what he did for humanity. Thus the church interposed not only between a person and God, but also between persons and in so doing sought to claim all service and absorb all social energies. Also deploring to

Rauschenbusch was that there was in the urban centers an increasing alienation between the working class and the churches. This was all the more evident wherever industrial development had advanced to the point of creating a distinct class of wage-workers. The traditional Protestant churches in the industrial urban centers were becoming the habitat almost exclusively of the managerial class and often moving to the suburbs with them, and the oppulence of these magnificent buldings reflected the life style of the affluent parishioners. The working man often no longer felt at home there; he could not relate to such evidences of wealth and could not appreciate the tone, the spirit, the point of view, which was that of another social class. The laborers were drifting away and becoming not only indifferent, but increasingly antagonistic to what mainline Protestantism was coming to represent.

Moving from an attempted restatement of Christian theology, passed an attack on urbanized mainline Protestantism, the professor analyzes what he considers to be the dechristianized spirit of capitalism. Though charged with naivete, he maintained that "business life is the unregenerate section of our social order," more so than other social organs. Claiming that it is hardly likely that any social revolution in the future will cause more "injustice, more physical suffering, and more heartache than the industrial revolution by which capitalism rose to power," he reasons that the inhumanity of capitalism is because "men learned to make wealth much faster than they learned to distribute it justly." Like many other observers of the scene, Rauschenbusch concedes that the technological advances being made far outstripped the advances being recorded in the development of humanity. He uses the analogy that "the eye for profit was keener than the ear for the voice of God and humanity." This he identifies as "the great sin of modern humanity and unless we repent, we shall perish by that sin." The reason is that "man is treated as a *thing* to produce more things. Men are hired as hands and not as men." He deplores that the laborers are paid only enough to maintain their working capacity, if indeed that, and not enough to develop their manhood; that they are subjected to frequent and prolonged layoffs; and that when their productive ability is exhausted they "are flung aside without consideration of their human needs." The unthrottled competitiveness of American business "pits men against one another in a gladiatorial game in which there is no mercy, and in which ninety per cent of the combatants finally strew the arena." This even extends to the children for "very early in life the children are hitched to the machine for life" with the result that "the vitality which ought to build their bodies during the crucial period of adolescence is used to make goods a little cheaper," or to state it slightly differently "to make profits a little larger." This reign of laissez faire economics Rauschenbusch concludes is a reign of fear; so that "the right to employment is the next great human right that demands recognition in public opinion and law." In a paraphrase of Psalm 139 is illustrated this condition and need:

Whither shall I go from thy hunger,
Or wheither shall I flee from thy greed?
If I ascend to the mountain forests, thou are there.
If I swing my pick in the mines, thou are there.
If I take the wings of the morning,
And emigrate to the uttermost coasts of the sea,
Even there shall thy hand seize me,
And thy right hand shall drain me.

As an antidote to this, Rauschenbusch suggests that wealth by extortion must cease and that work and service must become the sole title to income. To achieve this the immense powers of production must be taken from the ownership and control of a relatively small class of men. That such a small group has come to control American industrial life has not accelerated the human development but has in fact slackened the progress that could have been expected. This has happened because the social results brought forth by the common laborer have been appropriated primarily by the small oligarchy in control, and they have fortified these evil rights by unfair laws, throttled the masses by political centralization and suppression, and are consuming in luxury what they have taken in covetousness.

So it is that the avarice induced by our present economic system sacrifices the future of the race to immediate enrichment, and that mostly of the few. Strongly attacking the prevailing thought that all do indeed significantly participate in the advances of individual enterprise, Rauschenbusch came to advocate government ownership of coal mines and other natural resources, public ownership of railroads, waterways, gas and electric power, telegraph and telephone lines to insure far wider distribution of material advances.

Summarizing in his important study of 1907, Rauschenbusch made this analysis:

> The industrial and commercial life today is dominated by principles antagonistic to the fundamental principles of Christianity, and it is so difficult to live a Christian life in the midst of it that few men even try. If production could be organized on a basis of cooperative fraternity; if distribution could at least approximately be determined by justice; if all men could be conscious that their labor contributed to the welfare of all and that their personal well-being was dependent on the prosperity of the Commonwealth; if predatory business and parasitic wealth ceased and all men lived only by their labor; if the luxury of unearned wealth no longer made us all feverish with covetousness and a simpler life became the fashion; if our time and strength were not used up either in getting a bare living or in amassing unusable wealth and we had more leisure for the higher pursuits of the mind and the soul—then there might be a chance to live such a life of gentleness and brotherly kindness and tranquility of heart as Jesus desired for men.

What is the role of the Christian faith and the church in

this gigantic task? In general terms it is "to teach society to value human life more than property, and to value property only in so far as it forms the material basis for the higher development of human life." To this rather abstract statement Rauschenbusch made explicit and concrete suggestions, many of which were to be publically brought forth the next year in "the Social Creed of the Churches" adopted at the General Conference of the Methodist Church and then achieving wider influence when adopted by the newly founded Federal Council of Churches later in 1908. The statement asserted:

We deem it the duty of all Christian people to concern themselves directly with certain practical industrial problems. To us it seems that the churches must stand -

> For equal rights and complete justice for all men in all stations of life.
>
> For the right of all men to the opportunity for self-maintenance, a right ever to be wisely and strongly safeguarded against encroachments of every kind.
>
> For the right of workers to some protection against the hardships often resulting from the swift crises of industrial change.
>
> For the principle of conciliation and arbitration in industrial dissensions.
>
> For the protection of the worker from dangerous machinery, occupational disease, injuries and mortality.
>
> For the abolition of child labor.
>
> For such regulations of the conditions of toil for women as shall safeguard the physical and moral health of the community.
>
> For the suppression of the 'sweating system.'
>
> For the gradual and reasonable reduction of the hours of labor to the lowest practicable point, and for that degree of leisure for all which is a condition of the highest human life.
>
> For a release from employment one day in seven.

For a living wage as a minimum in every industry, and
for the highest wage that each industry can afford.

For the most equitable division of the products of industry that can ultimately be devised.

For suitable provision for the old age of the workers and
for those incapacitated by injury.

For the abatement of poverty.

Rauschenbusch contended that "a single frank and prayer-
ful discussion of such topics as these in a social meeting of the
church or its societies would create more social morality and
good custom than many columns in the newspapers." Also,
since "the Church has often rendered valuable aid by joining
the advanced public conscience of any period in its protest
against some single intolerable evil", here was a further challenge to the church to not just preach sermons, but to engage
the laity in forthright discussions of the major problems of
urban America; and in ways as these to bring about a Christianizing of public morality.

In 1912 Rauschenbusch could exalt in the public
expressions being made by many Protestant churches in the
pursuit of some form of the social gospel. He pointed out that
this stands in vivid contrast to the end of the nineteenth
century when advocates such as himself remember that as a
time of lonesomeness. He recalled that the few that there
were "used to form a kind of flying wedge to support a man
who was preparing to attack a ministers' conference with the
social Gospel." Then in 1912 he contended that "ministers
who were not already physically or mentally old by 1900,
and who were not rendered inpervious by doctrinal rubber-
coating of some kind, have been permeated by the social
interest almost in a body." So much was this the case that
young men preparing for the ministry frequently found the
social interest a serious rival of the old ministerial calling.
Some in fact turned to settlement house work, or the
YMCA as a more opportune location for social usefulness
than the pastorate of a church.

He applauded the publishing boards of several denominations for putting forth literature which expressed the most forward thought in the church on social questions; and he extolled that few seminaries of first-class standing did not have a chair devoted to "social ethics" or "Christian sociology". What had happened, however, was that the concept o the Kingdom of God had been laid aside in favor of a study of the ethical teachings of Jesus, and when this occurred the social gospel became official as denominations set up boards and commissions with paid staffs to study labor problems. In 1912 he could also commend many denominations for now having taken an active role in the propagandizing of social Christianity. The Episcopal Church had been the first American denomination to become actively involved even though it had failed to take an active leading role in older social conflicts, but was now being influenced by the very creative social movements then alive in the Church of England. The Department of Church and Labor in the Presbyterian Church with its friendly relations with orgainzed labor showed what leadership could do in a denomination that was considered conservative by reason of wealth, social standing, and doctrinal traditions. He did not note that this denomination had only very recently become active, and only after the American middle class had been aroused. He ignored the early role of the Congregationalists by only suggesting that they and the Baptists, Disciples, Unitarians and Universalists with their democratic governing principles appear to portent strong social gospel accents. The Methodist Church with its highly centralized organization and consistent constituency among the common people should also be a boon to the social gospel as its Social Creed already exhibited; again he failed to note that this denomination also had only recently become involved. Only the Lutherans among the mainline Protestant churches did not appear hopeful to Rauschenbusch. He lauded their institutional charities, but did not discern any trace that as a major American religious group they were sharing in the new social enthusiasm. A widely heralded interdenominational agent for social gospel concerns was the Men and Religion Forward Movement of 1911 and 1912. Rauschenbusch could say of this that "the movement had probably done more than any other single agency to lodge the social gospel in the common mind of the Church." Begun as a massive campaign to win three million Americans to the Church it became converted into a social gospel campaign. By 1917 he could say that the social gospel is no longer a prophetic and occasional note. "It is a novelty only in backward social or religious communities. The social gospel has become orthodox." In spite of this, the social gospel was "more a pulpit and platform movement than it was one devoted to social or political action."

The foremost exponent of the social gospel was so optimistic in 1912 that he proclaimed that the four great sections of our social order, namely, the family, the organized religious life, the institutions of education, and the political organization of the nation, had passed through constitutional changes which had made them at least to some degree part of the organism through which the spirit of Christ can do its work in humanity. This too suggests a reviving of the Puritan ideal of a thoroughly Christianized society as the gospel of wealth advocates also thought they were doing. In both cases it was a similarity in form and not in content. Some charged him with a naive outlook, but when World War I broke out two years later, he could refer back to previous writings where he had carefully stated that progress is much more than a natural thing. It is divine and no one nor no group can alone unquestionably chart the unbroken, forward progress of mankind. In that same year Rauschenbusch could point to a significant accomplishment of what the social gospel was about when the noted American industrialist, Henry Ford, announced that every worker employed by the Ford Motor Company who was over twenty-two years of age would be paid a minimum wage of five dollars a day, and this when production reached one thousand Model T's a day. In taking this action Ford observed that the rewards from industry had gone more heavily to capital than to labor, and then admitted that labor was entitled to a greater share. This electrified the social gospel advocates as well as the American laboring force. Yet, in a very definite way, men were being exhorted to be religious for the sake of civilization, and unconsciously for many social gospel advocates, not including Rauschenbusch, an idealized Americanism had become the real center of interest.

The foremost popularizer of social Christianity was the Rev. Charles M. Sheldon (1857-1946), who, while pastor of the Central Congregational Church, Topeka, Kansas, delivered a series of Sunday evening sermons that were incorporated into a novel published in 1897 under the title *In His Steps*. The novel, which is largely without literary merit, was nonetheless a panoramic view of much of American Protestantism and eventually sold in the millions of copies. Many Americans could identify with various characters in the narrative, and Sheldon portrayed them in such a way that they served as a challenge to optimistic American Protestants who believed it was indeed possible to build the kingdom of God on earth. It is not difficult for the reader of this novel to become swept up in the sentimentality of Sheldon's utopian vision that blends so well with the individual and corporate concept of perfectionism that had developed through nineteenth century American thought. The novel was only one of several literary endeavors that were attempts on the part of Sheldon to overcome the deep emotional experience he had his first year in Topeka observing the effects of serious unemployment as a result of the financial panic of 1893. Initially this led him to spend a week disguised as an unemployed laborer looking for work. The social conditions he discovered so shocked him that he continued his venture spending a total of nine weeks living incognito the lives of Topeka's eight principle social groups, and then sharing his experiences with his congregation and offering solutions on how to over-come the alienation of the classes which so disturbed him. Unlike much of the popular individualistic pietism running through American Protestantism, Sheldon was not con-cerned with recreating first century Christianity on the American soil. The thrust was not primitive Christianity in the sense of returning individual and church life to what was assumed to have been the golden era, and laid out in minute concrete detail in the historically accurate accounts of the New Testament. Instead the intention was to transplant Jesus from his rural Palestinian background of the first century A.D., and place him in the contemporary scene so that the essence of his teachings could find expression in this time and under these circumstances.

Bearing a subtitle "What Would Jesus Do?," the challenge of the book was to take a pledge to earnestly and honestly for an entire year not to do anything without first asking that question, and then after asking to follow Jesus exactly as one knows how, no matter what the results may be.

While there are several emphases in the book, the major thrust is the social gospel. This becomes evident immediate-ly, for as the story opens the Rev. Henry Maxwell, pastor of the affluent and prestigious First Church of Raymond, is put-ting the final touches on his Sunday morning sermon, and as he sits at his desk on Saturday morning he is interrupted by a knock on the door. Reluctantly answering, he is confronted by a shabbily dressed young man, who after a moment's pause, says: "I'm out of a job sir, and thought maybe you might put me in the way of getting something." Stating his inability to do so, and the fact that he was very busy, the minister wishes the young man well and closes the door on him and returns to finish polishing his sermon based on I Peter 2:21: "For hereunto were ye called; because Christ also suffered for you, leaving you an example, that ye should fol-low his steps."

The next morning at the conclusion of the eloquent presentation of this sermon in First Church, the same young man walks down the center aisle. To the startled congregation, he very calmly relates the story of his life over the past ten months. He tells how he has lost his job as a printer with the advent of the new linotype machines; and since that is the only trade he knows, he has been tramping all over the country in search of a new position. This has been fruitless, and now his health is broken, and as his wife has already died in a New York tenement his little daughter is staying with another prᵢₙter's family. He then asks the congregation just what it means to follow in the steps of Jesus and by rather direct implication, what is the responsibility of the wealthy members of this socially prominent congregation to the masses of poor and starving people breathing the feted air of the tenement districts. What indeed is to be the response to such a sermon as they have heard that morning and its recapitulation in the words of the soprano soloist:

Where He leads me I will follow,
I'll go with Him, with Him, all the way.

The young man then collapses and is carried to the minister's home where in spite of loving care he expires during the week.

The next Sunday morning when Mr. Maxwell addresses the congregation, it is immediately evident that the eloquent preacher that they have come to respect and admire is not standing before them; rather it is a man with a burden on his conscience that he earnestly wants to share with his congregation. Never having heard him speak in this manner, the congregation is further startled as he closes the sermon with an invitation to his listeners to meet with him after the service to discuss the possibilities of taking the pledge to walk in the steps of Jesus.

The first part of the novel consists of episodes of how various members of the congregation attempt to carry out the pledge, and, in biblical style, all but one, after much trial, remain faithful. The book then shifts the scene from the mythical Raymond to Chicago, where the experiment is also tried, but with several notable adaptations as the thrust of the story matures with experience.

At the initial meeting of those considering the pledge, the question arises as to the source of knowledge concerning what Jesus would do at the present time. The point is that "it is a different age. There are many perplexing questions in our civilization that are not mentioned in the teachings of Jesus." The answer to this fundamental inquiry is basic to much of American religious history; namely, the Spirit of Jesus will lead you into all truth. This bespeaks the thread running through American religious history so poignantly stated by the Rev. John Robinson to the Pilgrims on the eve of their departure for the New World: "the Lord hath more truth and light yet to break forth out of his holy Word." There were no strict guidelines, and each person had thus the responsibility on the basis of his own study of the Scriptures under the direct guidance of the Holy Spirit to perceive what the will of God is for him in his own specific circumstances. What a person determined to be right is probably the mind of Jesus, and is for him right; and each person was to have a sympathetic appreciation for the other's decision. It was assumed that while there might be minor variations, the essence of the teachings of Christ would be similiarly perceived.

Accenting the social gospel stance, the followers of Jesus in Raymond were not simply interested in treating the social ills they uncovered but were interested, as Maxwell stated "to remove the causes of such a condition." The followers were challenged to remake society according to what they perceived the will of God to be, and thus to inaugurate the kingdom of God in Raymond. The basic cause of the trouble in the world was stated in typical social gospel concepts: "It was suffering from selfishness." The answer to this was also very clear: "No one ever lived who had succeeded in overcoming selfishness like Jesus."

With the ardour and abandon of a new movement caught

up in the prospects of immediate success, the narrative un-
folds the experiences of several key people in the city, those
in managerial positions, who undertake the challenge. One
of the most prominent figures is Edward Norman, the owner
of the *Daily News*. He sets before himself the challenge to
treat every subject "from the standpoint of the advancement
of the kingdom of God on earth." As such he decides that
Jesus would not print the account of a championship boxing
match and a little later, that Jesus would not run ads for
alcoholic beverages. Revenues quickly drop and the owner is
confronted by his closest advisor, the managing editor, that
the paper will be bankrupt in thirty days if Norman runs the
paper "strictly on Christian principles" as he sees them. His
friend asserts that the theory is good, but that the world is
not ready for this, and will not support it. This then leads
Norman to call all his staff together for the first time, as he
thinks that Jesus would "probably run a newspaper on some
loving family plan, where editors, reporters, pressmen all
meet to discuss and devise and plan for the making of a
paper" that would carry out the announced Christian intention. Though the circulation continues to drop dramatically
and all suffer—from the newsboys who cannot sell, to the
highest level of management who cannot comprehend what
Norman is doing—the situation is finally saved by a
Carnegie-like action on the part of a millionaire heiress who
has also taken the pledge. She subscribes a half million dollars to underwrite a Christian newspaper in Raymond. This
is actualized in the experience of Sheldon when in 1900 an
effort was made to edit the *Topeka Daily Capital* just as Jesus
would have done it.

Another episode reflecting the thrust of social Christianity
is the account of the store owner, Milton Wright. He sets
forth a creed of what Jesus would probably do in Milton
Wright's place as a businessman:

1. He would engage in the business first of all for the
   purpose of glorifying God, and not for the primary
   purpose of making money.

2. All money that might be made He would never regard as His own, but as trust funds to be used for the good of humanity.

3. His relations with all the persons in His employ would be the most loving and helpful. He could not help thinking of all of them in the light of souls to be saved. This thought would always be greater than His thought of making money in the business.

Taking some of the ideas common to the gospel of wealth, Wright is depicted as adding the social gospel conviction that all persons are intended by God for salvation so that conduct of the business and the use of the trust funds should not be to aid a presumed elect few, but be used to enhance the life of all, with concern for their religious development being top priority. A move in this direction as perceived by social gospel advocates is seen in the question posed to Wright: "Does your plan contemplate what is coming to be known as co-operation?" His response is "Yes, as far as I have gone, it does."

Indicating the price some had to pay in adopting the pledge as their guiding principle is the case of Alexander Powers, the superintendent at the railroad yards. Inadvertently coming across interoffice correspondence that reveals the presence of violations of the recently established codes under the jurisdiction of the Interstate Commerce Commission, Powers is placed in a position of having to make a decision as to how seriously he has taken the pledge. If he reveals what he has uncovered, he will lose his position with the railroad, and this will mean serious financial loss, which, while not so devastating to him personally, will be traumatic for his socially prominent wife and daughter. In the spirit of the novel, Powers retains the integrity of the pledge and consequently suffers derision by his associates and observes the humiliation of his family. The whole incident is redeemed because before he read the devastating correspondence he had fitted out a large room at the yards to be used by the employees as a lunch and recreation room. To this room he had invited Mr. Maxwell to come and speak, and Mr. Maxwell had done so and been received surprisingly well. The author then observes that this "was the first plank laid down to help bridge the chasm between the church and labor in Raymond." Another concern of the social gospel had been concretized as a link is made between the institution of the church and the laboring man.

Writing in 1912, some fifteen years after the first appearance of the novel, Walter Rauschenbusch wrote despairingly of the work. While acknowledging that the writings of Sheldon have set "forth with winning spirit" the aims of the social gospel and thousands of young people have tried for a week to live as Jesus would, the fact of the matter is that Sheldon's objective "is so high a law that only consecrated individuals can follow it permanently and intelligently, and even they may submit to it only in the high tide of their spiritual life." The judgment of Rauschenbusch on the social gospel as a law is that it is "mainly useful to bring home the fact that it is hard to live a Christlike life in a mammonistic society. It convicts our social order of sin, but it does not reconstruct it." What Rauschenbusch is underscoring here is the basic Protestant concept of the sixteenth century Reformation that Christianity cannot be turned into a new law without bringing forth the same results of personal condemnation instead of redemption, while what is needed is a gospel which is a gift of God and has redeeming qualities.

This judgment is well deserved, and the basis for it is never fully addressed in the novel. The realization of the truth of the charge is implicit in that in an analysis of the experience in Raymond, a friend of Maxwell writes after a period of observation that the result of the pledge upon the congregation has been twofold. "On the one hand, it has brought a spirit of Christian fellowship which Maxwell tells never before existed, and which now impresses him as being very nearly what Christian fellowship of the apostolic churches must have been, and would seem to be an accurate under-, standing of the gospel." The other result, however, is that "it has divided the church into two distinct groups of members." This division is not seen by Sheldon as unfortunate, for it has catalyzed Maxwell to think that "the Christianity of our times must represent a more literal imitation of Jesus, and especially in the element of suffering."

This is distressing to Rauschenbusch who rejoins: "No man is a follower of Jesus in the full sense who has not through him entered into the same life with God. But on the other hand no man shares his life with God whose religion does not flow out, naturally and without effort, into all relations of his life and reconstructs everything that it touches." Suffering therefore is not a goal of religion. Rauschenbusch disagrees with the thrust of the first part of *In His Steps* wherein the accent is on the individual reconstructing society from the management level down and suffering much in the process; instead, he calls attention to the fact that such an approach must also be complimented by a message that persuades the individuals, as individuals, that there is indeed a better way of life. Rauschenbusch insists that Christianity is a gospel to be proclaimed, not a law to be obeyed.

Such a possibility did seem available in the Socialist Party; and both Sheldon and Rauschenbusch underscore the diffi-culty of many of their contemporaries in separating their understanding of Christianity and socialism, and are fearful the former may lead naturally to the latter. Sheldon discusses the problem in a statement made by a Socialist leader: "I don't look for any reform worth anything to come out of the churches." He then cries out: "They are not with the people. They are with the aristocrats, with the men of money. The trusts and monopolies have their greatest men in the churches. The ministers as a class are their slaves." He calls for a system that will start from the common basis of social-ism founded on the rights of the common people, and de-clares that this is to be accomplished with a new start in the way of government. This sets Maxwell to thinking as Sheldon challenges the reader to be wary that the church may have "lost its power over the very kind of humanity which in the early days of Christianity it reached in the greatest numbers." The question raised is if the church is so removed from its Master that people no longer can find Him there. Rauschenbusch also shows similar concern when he notes that many clergymen and churchmen do not challenge the present situation, because they honestly see nothing wrong, and have "never had a vision from God to shake their illusions." He then admits that under such conditions some of "the pioneers of the social gospel have had a hard time trying to consolidate their old faith and their new aim." For some this has been an ideological struggle and some have lost their faith and others have "come out of the struggle with crippled formulations of truth," such as Henry Demarest Lloyd, known for *Wealth Against Commonwealth*, his passionate indictment of Standard Oil, who proclaimed in 1903: "Christianity is the religion that was, Socialism is the religion that is to be." Rauschenbusch also acknowledges that "socialism has laid hold of the industrial working class with the grip of destiny," and while it is seemingly working at cross purposes with Christianity and has ensnared some sensitive Christian leaders, he faces the future with optimism. He concludes that "God had to raise up Socialism because the organized church was too blind, or too slow, to realize God's end," but "aside from the dangers involved in party orthodoxy we may safely trust that Socialism will slough off its objectionable elements as it matures," and then "those qualities against which the spirit of genuine Christianity justly protests are not of the essence of Socialism." The conclusion to be reached from this is that the socialism of today, will not be the socialism of tomorrow; and that it will eventually find its true home within the bounds of the social Christianity as taught by Jesus and hopefully adequately expressed in the church. Josiah Strong's contention that "Socialism attempts to solve the problem of suffering without eliminating the factor of sin," will be met by the more perceptive insights of the Christian faith when it is realized that you cannot regenerate society without first regenerating the individual, and only then can a co-operative society replace a highly competitive one. It must be noted that the Socialist Party reached its greatest influence in the election of 1912, and after that went into a noted decline. Also such optimism as the social gospel articulated was not to find as compatible an age after the close of World War I. Other interests then came to the fore, and the social gospel movement, never as popular as Rauschenbusch and other devoted followers thought, went into a decline in the latter twenties.

3

The Urban Impact

During the half century following the Civil War, the American people felt the full impact of the country's ethnic and religious pluralism as masses of immigrants streamed into the country in a seemingly endless onrush, a total of twenty-five million persons between 1860 and 1917. During the decade of 1901-1910 alone, a total of 8,795,386 immigrants entered the country. In terms of religious convictions, there was by no means a unanimity of opinion; but a basic element of the newly arrived cultural baggage was a tenacious tie to his European culture which, at times, included a church tradition. These cultural roots he was very reluctant to give up and attempted to transmit them to his children and grandchildren. The church tradition may have been quite a different matter. Numerous immigrants who belonged to various European state churches wished to continue these affiliations in America, and their native loyalties led them to seek out or at least be receptive to representatives of their home church. Others sought to maintain the religious tradition, albeit it, in some reformed way, and were amenable to a somewhat altered form of the old faith being institutionalized in a new church in this country. Others were sectarians who had broken away from their homeland religious institutions, and who sought in America the greater freedom to pursue their own religious convictions. Others sought to throw off the religious affiliations of the past and to seek a new religious home on the American scene. Still others were at best, nominal adherents to some state church, and were opened to its influence as a cultural tie. Then there were those who were anticlerical in tone, especially from the urban areas of Europe, who were eager in this land of religious freedom to finally be able to be relieved of any religious associations or harassments.

Religious forces were thus faced with a multiple challenge in gathering these millions of immigrants in one religious institution or another; and among the most serious challenges to this mission were the urban centers that were rapidly developing after the Civil War.

During the forty year period, from 1860 to 1900, the population distribution of the United States went from six million out of thirty million living in towns and cities with more than 2,500 residents to thirty million out of seventy-six million being urbanized. By 1917 the nation's population of slightly over one hundred million was equally divided between rural and urban concentrations. By the 1890's it was to the cities that most of the immigrants were flocking, and by the turn of the century, the work force in any industry relying heavily on unskilled labor looked to these immigrants for such workers.

Some fifteen years earlier there had been a marked shift in the origins of the immigrants. Prior to 1885, the immigrants had come primarily from the British Isles, Germany, or the Scandinavian countries; but after that time an increasing number came from Southern, Eastern and Southeastern Europe. Representing different cultures, crowding into cities as the frontier closed, these new settlers were victimized by a mythology that quickly grew up characterizing them as undesirable aliens who would only lead to the corruption of the nation. Viewed contemptuously by the "older Americans" and exploited by economic organizers, their life in the American cities was indeed a harsh one. So it was that an astute observer could state: "The city is the nerve center of our civilization. It is also the storm center."[1]

Vividly portraying in word and picture the conditions of the immigrant slums of New York City was Jacob A. Riis. A twenty-one year old Danish immigrant to the United States in 1870, Riis arrived just as economic conditions were beginning to worsen, becoming particularly severe as a result of the 1873 depression. He experienced the precariousness and degradation of the unfortunate immigrant, often himself being jobless, hungry, and homeless. For months he searched in vain for work; but in 1877 became a police reporter for the New York *Tribune*. Working out of the police headquarters on Mulberry Street in the very heart of the East side slum district, he became thoroughly acquainted with the prevelant conditions which brought forth in him both compassion and indignation. His daily stories in the *Tribune* contributed greatly to the initiation of programs of reform; but his books, beginning with *How the Other Half Lives* in 1890, impressed upon the American people the urgent need of positive action. Even though he expressed prejudice and was guilty of stereotyping immigrant groups, as well as not always being able to see the advances made in the slums, he characterized all too accurately the plight of the urban immigrant.

He stated in regard to New York that three-fourths of its people in 1890 lived in tenements, and that the continuing influx further crowded the situation. He also observed that: "Its poverty, its slums, and its suffering are the result of unprecedented growth with the consequent disorder and crowding, and the common penalty of metropolitan greatness." With the observation that the people will live near their work, he knew that the densely populated areas were there to stay. He characterized the scene by quoting a report of the Society for the Improvement of the Condition of the Poor: "Crazy old buildings, crowded rear tenements in filthy yards, dark, damp basements, leaking garrets, shops, outhouses, and stables converted into dwellings, though scarcely fit to shelter brutes, are habitations of thousands of our fellow beings in this wealthy, Christian city."

Technically what was a tenement? Riis gives the legal definition: A house "occupied by three or more families, living independently and doing their cooking on the premises; or by more than two families on a floor, so living and cooking and having a common right in the halls, stairways, yards, etc." In reality, a working definition would be: "It is generally a brick building from four to six stories high on the street, frequently with a store on the first floor which, when used for the sale of liquor, has a side opening for the benefit of the inmates and to evade the Sunday law; four families occupy each floor, and a set of rooms consists of one or two dark closets, used as bedrooms, with a living room twelve by ten. The staircase is too often a dark well in the center of the house, and no direct through ventilation is possible, each family being separated from the other by partitions." In 1890, Riis, using somewhat inaccurate statistics, declared that 1,250,000 lived in 37,316 such structures in New York City. Observing that these places were inhabited almost entirely by immigrant families, he traced the recent history of the slums: "The once unwelcome Irishman has been followed in his turn by the Italian, the Russian Jew, and the Chinaman, and has himself, taken a hand at opposition, quite as bitter and quite as ineffectual, against these later hordes." These people have no other place to live. "They are truly poor for having no better homes; waxing poorer in purse as the exorbitant rents to which they are tied, as ever was serf to soil, keep rising." A typical example was described as a family of nine: "husband, wife, an aged grandmother, and six children; honest, hard-working Germans. All nine lived in two rooms, one about ten foot square, that served as parlor, bedroom, and eating room. The rent was seven dollars and a half a month, more than a week's wages for the husband."

In attending a meeting of all denominations to discuss the question as to how to lay hold of these teeming masses with

Christian influences, he heard one speaker say: "How shall the love of God be understood by those who have been nurtured in sight only of the greed of man?" It was pointed out that rent as well as prices for nearly all the staples of life were much higher in the slums than in any other part of the city. Riis agitated for what he was convinced was an economic fact: that if absentee landlords would have been willing to take less of an immediate profit, the long range financial gain would, in the end, have been far greater. However, most landlords operated under the principle: "Collect the rent in advance, or failing, eject the occupants." The assumption was that these people, of which there was no shortage, do not have the ability to take care of a more decently appointed apartment. Yet Riis was quick to point out: "The poorest immigrant comes here with the purpose and ambition to better himself and, given half a chance, might be reasonably expected to make the most of it. To the false plea that he prefers the squalid homes in which his kind are housed there could be no better answer. The truth is, his half chance has too long been wanting, and for the bad result he has been unjustly blamed." It was indeed a vicious circle that entrapped millions.

Fortunately there was often another aspect of this narrative: "A story of thousands of devoted lives, laboring earnestly to make the most of their scant opportunities for good; of heroic men and women striving patiently against fearful odds and by their very courage coming off victors in the battle with the tenement; of womanhood pure and undefiled. That it should blossom in such an atmosphere is one of the unfathomable mysteries of life." In acknowledging this to be the case, he did not seek to document it as did the more optimistically minded Bishop Lawrence writing about conditions in Boston in 1901: "Watch the cartloads of Polish or Italian immigrants as they are hauled away from the dock. Study their lifeless expression, their hangdog look, and their almost cowering posture. Follow them and study them five years later: note the gradual straightening of the body, the kindling of the eye, and the alertness of the whole person as the men, women, and children begin to realize their opportunities, bring in their wages, and move to better quarters. Petty temptations and deep degradations that might have overwhelmed them on their arrival cannot touch them now."

Riis would rather accent that living under conditions that were freezing in the winter and unbearably hot in the summer the tenement dweller lived on, though in the midst of a death rate that was astoundingly high, especially among the children; but he also observed that perhaps the greatest threat to life was the ever-present saloon. This is portrayed in an interrogation of a boy at the police station:

"Where do you go to church, my boy?"
"We don't have no clothes to go to church."
"Well, where do you go to school then?"
"I don't go to school," with a snort of contempt.
"Where do you buy your bread?"
"We don't buy no bread; we buy beer."

Riis lamented: "Turn and twist it as we may, over against every bulwark for decency and morality which society erects, the saloon projects its colossal shadow, omen of evil wherever it falls into the lives of the poor." "To their misery it sticketh closer than a brother, persuading them that within its doors only is refuge, relief. It has the best of the argument, too, for it is true, worse pity, that in many a tenement-house block the saloon is the one bright and cheery and humanly decent spot to be found. It is a sorry admission to make, that to bring the rest of the neighborhood up to the level of the saloon would be one way of squelching it; but it is so." He goes on to write "Wherever the tenements thicken, it multiplies. Upon the direst poverty of their crowds it grows fat and prosperous, levying upon it a tax heavier than all the rest of its grievous burdens combined."

What was to be done amongst teeming masses that worked twelve and more hours a day in their desperate efforts to maintain family unity, and often failed; that lived in an area crowded with thieves, pimps, prostitutes, gangsters, beggars and all other forms of criminal life that proved enticing to the youth. Riis summed it up this way: "You cannot expect to find an inner man to appeal to in the worst tenement-house surroundings. You must first put the man where he can respect himself. To reverse the argument of the apple: you cannot expect to find a sound core in a rotten fruit."

How were the Protestant churches to respond to this scene when they did not have much of an American experience upon which to draw? True, there were some European antecedents, especially in the Church of England, and studies were made of various attempts being made in England and also in Germany to meet the crisis of the urban setting.

One of the studies made of the American scene was initiated in 1865 to determine how the energy devoted in wartime service to the soldiers could now be redirected to peacetime service in the cities. As a result the wartime United States Christian Commission became that autumn the American Christian Commission to help develop a systematic program for urban missions. The task of the organization was to ascertain actual conditions prevailing in the cities and to assemble information concerning what had been done to combat the problem. In the study undertaken in thirty-five cities it was discovered that while piecemeal work was being done, there was no overall urban strategy. It was suggested the time tested approach of personal visitation be undertaken whereby church members would make house to house visitations to the non-churched in all parts of the city. This program was not successfully implemented; so the next suggestion was to hire women missionaries to do this same work, somewhat on the pattern of German deaconesses. This, despite initial hostility, met with modest success. Through this program it was learned that there frequently were no Protestant churches in the areas of greatest need; for example it was later documented that from 1868 to 1888 seventeen Protestant churches moved out of the district below Fourteenth Street, New York, while two hundred thousand more people crowded into this area. In 1880 New York had one evangelical (Protestant) church for every three thousand residents; but ten years later it was one for every four thousand people, whereas across the country it was one Protestant church for every 438 people. In the heart of Chicago in the 1880's sixty thousand had no church whatsoever. While this did not lead to the establishment of many new Protestant congregations, it did lend considerable support to the developing pattern of conventional institutional mission undertakings, and the training of individuals to staff them.

One of the outstanding developments in this urban outreach was that led by the new social workers in what were called the Settlement Houses. A famous example of this was Hull House established by Jane Addams in Chicago in 1889 or Graham Taylor's Chicago Commons. These neighborhood centers with their day nurseries, gymnasiums and classes, including language courses became an attempt through instruction to raise the urban poor above the morass in which they had been forced to live. This was in the tradition of the rural individualistic stance of American Protestantism: to address social problems by setting up some voluntary association to implement a rescue program for the unfortunate victims; but now at the same time to also become laboratories to study the social conditions of the day. Hull House received little clerical support, and was under ministerial attack for its lack of religious education so that Miss Addams maintained a friendly though critical relation with social gospel advocates.

Illustrating this undertaking as a distinctly Christian form of endeavor is Charles Sheldon in the second part of *In His Steps*. In this portion of the book the challenge to live as Jesus would is taken from Raymond to Chicago where after an attempt is made by the pastor of the Nazareth Avenue

Church to introduce and carry out a program similar to that attempted earlier at Raymond, the accent shifts to the experience of that pastor, his good friend, the bishop, and a young girl whose family wealth had suddenly been wiped out by the failure of her father's business speculations, as these individuals become active in the founding and operating of a settlement house in a Chicago slum. The novel climaxes in this specific example of institutionalized social Christianity, as the point is made of "the hatred of the church by countless men who see in it only great piles of costly stone, and upholstered furniture and the minister as a luxurious idler." Here in this venture the Christian life is not one of righting one's own life and imposing a new style on others, but by immersing oneself in the lives of the ghetto residents seeking not only overtly to proclaim the gospel, but by living out its implications in the teaching of crafts, housekeeping and cooking; seeking by persuasion as well as example to rescue individuals from the saloon and aiding them in securing adequate housing and positions of responsibility to enhance personal dignity. The novel thus closes on a note of the penetration of the good news of the Gospel into concentrated areas of urban blight.

Especially attractive examples of this are seen in the young woman's opening of houskeeping classes to train local residents for employment in other parts of the city, thus allowing the slum girls a chance to leave their familiar environment for the more pleasant sections of the city, and at the same time to earn their own livelihood and thus perhaps escape the slums that Riis felt was so hard to do. Also underscoring an argument put forth by Riis is the scene portrayed by Sheldon of the reaction of a Christian absentee landlord to the story of the death of an unemployed father shot in a coal yard stealing fuel to heat a tenement room in this man's building. The conscience of the landlord is touched, and he sets in motion a plan to upgrade the quality of his apartments, which will not only bring more pleasant living accommodations for the tenants, but in the long run a greater revenue for the investor. Riis' complaints about the power of the saloon are also a major point of this section of Sheldon's book. He tells the story of how a man had tried unsuccessfully to renounce the hold of alcohol over him, and while also continuing a life of crime, he unknowingly held up the bishop in a darkened alley. Then in hearing the bishop's voice he refuses to take the cherished watch he was trying to loosen from the bishop's vest, because of the efforts the bishop had made on his behalf some years before. The bishop then takes him to the settlement house and gives him a job as a janitor and promises to aid him in his war against alcohol. It is a hard battle and the man is overcome by the fumes emanating from the nearby saloon while sweeping the settlement house steps. Fortunately the bishop appears on the scene and forcibly restrains him from entering the saloon. Indicative of the time, this story concludes upon an optimistic note when the owner of the saloon property, who had taken the pledge to walk in the steps of Jesus at the Nazareth Avenue Church, is persuaded to not renew the financially lucrative lease. Instead, the building was turned over to become an extension of the settlement house, in fact, to house the young lady's housekeeping classes.

The settlement house, as thus depicted by Sheldon, became a means of personal witness to the urban tenement dweller and his society. Sheldon, speaking on behalf of such men and women, deplored that individuals were not willing to give of themselves, but only with the surplus of their wealth would they support various charities, some of which became directly related to settlement house endeavors. Riis had commented less than a decade earlier that there was not a city on the earth as generous as New York in the supplying of funds for benevolent undertakings on behalf of the less fortunate. The net result was that though some consciences were pricked, the cost of such affliction, while significant in total dollars, was not injurious to the way of life for the contribu-

tor. Nonetheless this became an arm of mainline Protestantism as it rather haltingly sought to address the severe
problem that lay so close at hand.

Appearing shortly before the settlement house was the
institutional church. Though establishments of this kind were
rather limited in numbers, modifications of the program have
continued to be a basic element in much congregational
planning to the present time. One definition of such a church
is: "an organized body of Christian believers, who, finding
themselves in a hard and uncongenial social environment,
supplement the ordinary methods of the gospel—such as
preaching, prayer meetings, Sunday School, and pastoral
visitation—by a system of organized kindness, a congeries of
institutions, which by touching people on physical, social,
and intellectual sides, will conciliate them and draw them
within reach of the gospel."[2] In the boisterous and growing
mining city of Butte, Montana, a denominational executive
declared in 1902 that there was a great need for a well equipped and strongly supported institutional church, "which will
meet the intellectual and social, as well as the religious
demands of the thousands who are continually surrounded
by temptation in its most attractive and most dangerous
forms." In the following year the Episcopal church announced the opening of men's clubrooms. Here men could
come to read, play games, or box; the purpose was to raise
the moral standards of the men, and then by this method lead
them into the worshipping life of the congregation. While
this latter purpose remained to the fore, other forms of recreation and moral uplift were frequently provided such as
music groups, drama clubs, sewing circles, cooking schools,
day nurseries, language classes and other vehicles to take the
people in the industrial ghettos out of places of questionable
amusements and off the streets and to involve them in
wholesome forms of recreation; and self-improvement programs became widely known. Operating under the motto:
"open church doors every day and all the day," the move-

ment thought it had the answers to bringing a Christian influence to bear in areas where it was acknowledged to have little hearing. However, the program did not succeed to the degree that had been hoped; and its failure was not only due to the people taking advantage solely of the recreational and self-improvement aspects, but to the enormous cost of such programs. In fact, only if there were wealthy patrons willing to underwrite such ventures did the institutional church program usually even get started, let alone be maintained for any length of time. There were just not enough Morgans, Vanderbilts and Rockefellers to sustain this venture, which was an expression of mainline Protestantism to stay in changing neighborhoods and to reach out to the unchurched masses surrounding the church on the basis of a rather traditional institutional approach, even though acknowledged as having some creative programming. This approach, like that of the settlement house, acknowledged that there were serious problems, and sought to answer them by imposing the ideals of middle class society as the ultimate Christian accomplishment. Yet, the story of Russell Conwell's Baptist Temple in Philadelphia or Saint Bartholomew's or St. George's Protestant Episcopal Churches in New York present individual stories of statistical success. At Saint Bartholomew's the program was so large and varied that it took a three hundred and fifty page yearbook to describe the activities held there. This included over eight thousand meetings of various types in a year's time, the average number of gatherings on Sundays being nineteen and on weekdays twenty-four. With numerous services of worship in several languages on Sunday, each night was also the occasion for an evangelistic service. In addition to the usual clubs and classes there was an excellent medical clinic, an employment bureau and a loan association that sought to speak to immediate needs.

A variation of this movement is the city mission program, known more popularly as the Rescue Mission. This was a non-denominational approach begun in New York in 1872 with the founding of the Water Street Mission which offered derelicts food and shelter in addition to fervid preaching which was an attempt to guide them to reclamation and a life of usefulness. The movement spread across the nation leading to the development of a national organization in 1913 called the International Union of Gospel Missions.

Not all of the people crowding into the cities were European immigrants. Many were young men and some young women from the rural areas and small towns of America. These people, representing the "older American" stock, were of immediate and special concern to the Protestant churches. An analysis of their character and hope was also included by Riis in his *How the Other Half Lives.* He reports that the metropolis draws people like a lighted candle does the moth. Continuing the analogy he notes that "it attracts them in swarms that come year after year with the vague idea that they can get along here if anywhere; that something is bound to turn up among so many." It is then revealed that nearly all are young men, unsettled in life, and that many if not most of them are fresh from good homes and with honest hopes of getting a start in the city and making a way for themselves. Having little money to tide them over while they seek employment and having even less knowledge of the city and its pitfalls they are attracted to the inexpensive lodgings. "They have come in search of crowds, of life, and they gravitate naturally to the Bowery, the great democratic highway of the city, where the twenty-five-cent lodging-houses take them in." Here Riis points out that they come into contact with three distinct classes of associates: the great mass of adventurers like themselves, waiting there for something to turn up; a much smaller class of respectable clerks or mechanics, who, too poor or too lonely to have a home of their own, live this way from year to year; and lastly the thief in search of recruits for his trade. It is this third category that is so dangerous to the recent arrival.

Often the sights the young stranger sees and the company

he keeps are not of a kind to strengthen any moral principle he may have brought away from home. Then by the time his money is spent and he has as yet no work he is forced to seek cheaper lodgings. Then it is that so frequently he takes his abode in the fifteen-cent lodging house and he is ready for the tempter who awaits him there. Here among the ex-convicts just out of the prisons after having served time for robbery or theft, the opportunity the young man has been waiting for appears. He is enticed to join one of these gangs and enters upon a career of lawlessness.

To counter this tendency there was at hand an organization of the Protestant churches, namely, the Young Men's Christian Association. The YMCA had been organized in London in 1844 to improve "the spiritual condition of the young men engaged in the drapery and other trades." Once again the American Protestant churches were fortunate in being able to draw upon the resources of the English Christian community as it had creatively sought to meet the challenges of the industrialism that had earlier enveloped the island through a voluntary lay organization that sought to serve as an auxiliary to the churches, and not to be a denomination in itself, or particularly related to any one church. Dwight L. Moody, a prime mover of the Chicago YMCA and long time advocate for the "Y" stated: "Fifty or one hundred years ago young men lived at home. They lived in a country home, and did not come to these large cities and centers of commerce as they do now. If they did come, their employers took a personal interest in them. I contend that they do not do so now." He went on to say that "these young men who come to large cities want somebody to take an interest in them," and he asserted that this was the purpose and opportunity for the YMCA. This was being carried out as stated in the charter of the first American YMCA, that of Boston, in 1851. Herein the "Y" was described as "a social organization of those in whom the love of Christ has produced love to men; who shall meet the young stranger as he enters our city, take him by the hand, direct him to a boarding house where he may find a quiet home pervaded with Christian influence, introduce him to the church and the Sabbath School, bring him to the Rooms of the Association, and in every way throw around him good influences, so that he may feel that he is not a stranger, but that noble and Christian spirits care for his soul." Helping provide clean housing at very reasonable rates and establishing reading rooms and appropriate lectures, the "Y" sought to surround young men with a Christian environment that would enhance the character they brought with them and would aid them in developing themselves in the very opposite direction from that described by Riis. Very early asserting the policy of "a home away from home" this form of nurture aided the program of Bible classes to mature the Christian character of these strangers to the city.

As the "Y" developed to combat the constant thrust of temptation to these young men unaccustomed to being away from home and living in the unfamiliar urban environment, it established a program to strengthen the social, mental and physical capacities of its members, as well as the spiritual life, and sought to do so in a YMCA building specifically designed for this multiple purpose, with a staff especially trained to carry out the several objectives. It was the determination of the organization that its presence be felt in a community by a choice location so that its building stood at the crossroads of traffic. The organization enjoyed wide support from the mainline Protestant churches; also business corporations were strongly interested in supporting such movement for the cultivation of the type of character that they saw essential to the perpetuation of the "Christian-Capitalist Society." One of Sheldon's characters, Alexander Powers, the railroad superintendent, underscored this: "It is one of the contradictions of the railroad world that YMCA and other Christian influences are encouraged by the roads, while all the time the most unchristian and lawless acts may be committed in the official management of the roads themselves." Again the concern was to protect the values and ideals of the popular middle class society that was assumed by those who held power in it to be the most Christian society yet to be developed. However the "Y" in cities like New York and Chicago also had branches in the slum areas designed to be of service to the poor.

It was not only the young men that were coming to the cities, for the industrial development also offered economic possibilities for young women who sought release from the drudgery and loneliness of the farms or who helped their immigrant husbands support their large families. Their advancement was consistently hampered by the prevailing attitude that they need not be paid as much as men even for doing the same work. This practice long held the young women in economic bondage. Nonetheless, having to work longer hours and still being paid less did not deter them, and soon women in significant numbers were to be found where manufacturing processes were turned into pressing treadles or adjusting levers. Somewhat better off were the young ladies who qualified to be salesgirls, typists, and secretaries, and as the telephone became popular to be switchboard operators. Also very popular and respectable for a young woman was the position of schoolteacher. There was far more for a young lady to do than be a domestic as trained in the settlement house by Sheldon's character.

The response of the Protestant churches to this development was to show continual concern for the moral well being of the ladies and the community at large. While the rural and small town girls were considered a positive asset to the business world in most instances, they were also viewed as a potential danger to the moral well-being of the community. Thus it was that business and church organizations took considerable care in providing well-guarded residences for these girls of the older American stock. The working conditions and the sleeping quarters of the immigrant women were not the objects of such solicitude. Though not on the scale of the YMCA, the YWCA, stemming from the England of the 1850's, did seek to reach young women of varied backgrounds and experiences. While offering basic services such as providing food and lodging and operating employment bureaus, the chief goals came to be the cultivation of the "physical, social, intellectual, moral and spiritual interests of young women." Group programs for Christian study and fellowship enjoyed high priority, and a national organization was effected in 1906.

Another import from England was the Salvation Army, which became a distinctive denomination with a special concern for the urban poor. Like the Methodist Society in the eighteenth century, the Salvation Army in the nineteenth century organized within English Protestantism, but to effectively carry out its challenge ultimately found it necessary to cut loose from previous religious institutionalism and strike out on its own. The movement began in London in 1865, reorganized as the Salvation Army with the first introduction of its military trappings in 1878, and came to the United States in 1880. The founder, William Booth, had developed an evangelism technique in seeking to reach London's poor that included informal and colloquial sermons that were combined with ministering to the physical needs of his hearers. Such innovations as the use of brass bands and religious songs set to popular tunes were not planned, but developed naturally as the program developed. About the time the movement spread to America it developed, in addition to the basic idea of the corps, its uniform and flag. Upon arriving in America as well as in other parts of the world greater and greater emphasis was placed on the social aspects of its work. The Army was possibly best known for its Slum Brigades, which went into run-down areas, held services in saloons and halls, brought relief to the destitute and preached against vice. As a result the Army established food depots, homes for girls, industrial homes where men rebuilt their character, hospitals, low-cost lodging houses, nurseries for infants of working mothers, fresh-air camps, boy's clubs, and welfare work programs for prisoners. It was severely opposed at first, and its street meetings were ridiculed and harassed; but it was to be given recognition by mainline Protestant churches as frequently being able to witness the Gospel among the cold and hungry more effectively than they could.

Mainline denominations also established foreign language churches to attempt to incorporate the immigrants into the mainstream of American popular Christianity. While elaborate attempts were made to thus Americanize even the religion of the immigrants, large numbers were not converted, their religious life becoming the focus of the European ethnic churches at work in America.

In spite of all these attempts, Protestantism did not come up with adequate or satisfactory new forms for urban ministries. The traditional patterns simply were not abandoned or significantly altered; and it was the prospering middle class and the wealthy entrepreneur that the Protestant churches found in their pews. Henry Ward Beecher recognized this in 1874 and said of the churches in New York and Brooklyn: "it will be found that the aristocratic and prosperous elements have possession of them, and if the great under-class, the poor and needy, go to them at all, they go sparsely, and not as to a home." Not overly disturbed by this observation, Beecher went on to conclude: "our churches are largely for the mutual insurance of prosperous families, and not for the upbuilding of the great underclass of humanity."

Thus it is necessary to turn to the Roman Catholic Church to note how it responded to the gigantic waves of immigration, beginning with the Irish potato famines in the 1840's, to note how Christian forces most successfully met the urban impact in the half century following the Civil War. It has frequently been noted that the most spectacular development in American religious life during the latter half

of the nineteenth century was the growth of Roman Catholicism. Having a membership of approximately three and a
half million in 1865, this number increased to a figure
approaching eighteen million at the close of World War I. In
comparative figures what this means is that by 1920 every
sixth person in the United States was a Roman Catholic, or to
put it another way, one-third of those claiming church affiliation were members of the Roman faith. The great bulk of
these people were located in the urban centers of American
life.

Church statistics are notoriously inaccurate; and a debate
has occurred over whether or not the Roman Catholic
Church's growth, marked of course by natural increase, but
basically in the last thirty years of the nineteenth and first
twenty of the twentieth century accelerated by immigration,
represents an ability to retain its claim on those who naturally had an affiliation with it. A major study, though
somewhat disputed, argues that the vast Catholic immigration into the United States during the century from 1820 to
1920 was successfully assimilated and retained by the
American Church.[3] It is claimed that there is no evidence of
an enormous loss to the faith, and there is not even evidence
of a measurable loss during that period. The strength of the
Church in 1920 was due to immigration, and without that the
Church would likely have been what it was in 1790, a weak,
anemic body unable to make much impact on the country.

The heavy German immigration in the closing decades of
the century was replaced by large numbers from Italy,
Austria-Hungary and Poland in the early decades of the
twentieth century. For these non-English speaking peoples
representing cultures not widely found in the United States
there was a considerable cultural shock to be experienced
upon arrival. Students of immigration history have pointed
out that the more thorough the separation from the other
aspects of the old life, the greater at times was the hold of the
religion that alone survived the transfer. In the struggle to

save something of the familiar, some of the immigrants found refuge in their religious traditions and placed here the whole weight of their desire to remain connected to the traditions of their way of life. What this meant was the transfer of the old religious system to the New World. This meant not just the Gospel and the priest who proclaimed it and officiated at the significant turning points in a person's life, but also the holidays, processions, ancient customs, traditional rites, in effect, the whole life of the religion at home. In this way the religious outlook became increasingly conservative and with it a rigidity and abhorrence of change. In fact, the immigrants in America became far more conservative then their countrymen in Europe. This was particularly true among such large ethnic groups as the Germans and Poles. It was not so true among the Italians who were more likely to retain a nominal relationship to the church, a reflection of the adamant anticlericalism that had attended the unification of Italy and its aftermath; and also reflects the fact many Italian immigrants were unmarried young men who were not natural preservers of religious traditions, or were married men whose families remained in Italy while the father worked to earn money for them in the New World.

Among those who sought to preserve religious traditions, this conservative spirit within the Church was quickly encapsulated in the rapid development of the traditional diocesan structure of the Church. A major factor in the Church's success in retaining its membership was its ability to introduce as quickly as the need arose the organizational presence of the Church that had stood it in such good stead through the centuries. Unlike much of Protestantism which was scattered across the vast reaches of the country, the more compact Catholic centers permitted the old European diocesan structure to be implemented with continuing success, as is evidenced in the erection of some sixty dioceses between 1860 and the outbreak of World War I.

This conservative nature of the Catholic immigrant and

the ability of the Church to retain the millions of immigrants allowed Pope Pius X in 1908 to remove the Catholic Church in America from the supervision of the Congregation de Propaganda Fide by declaring that the United States was no longer to be considered a mission territory, but rather the Church here was to be considered on a par with the churches in the old Catholic nations of Europe.

This remarkable success story in numerical growth was not accomplished without considerable difficulty. There was the problem of staffing the churches. Fortunately large, though insufficient, numbers of priests, lay brothers and nuns came from several European countries, particularly Ireland, Germany, France and Belgium. Not only did they come in large numbers, but they came organized in specific orders and societies which not only made discipline possible, but under capable administration permitted an efficient deployment of the available staff to areas of need. Also advantageous to the American scene was that several Roman Catholic Missionary Societies, such as the Ludwig Missionsverein of Bavaria, the Leopoldinen Stiftung in Austria and the Societie de Propagande de Fide in France had financial resources to greatly aid in the support of the work in America. The problem of finances was an acute one on the American scene as not only were the Catholic immigrants initially poor, and remained this way for some time; they had little experience in the voluntary support of religious institutions. Accustomed to the practice of the Church supporting itself by grants from the state or from the income of its own lands it was a painful lesson that if they wished the Church that they would have to largely fund it themselves. So much time and energy of the clergy had to be expended in the raising of funds that they ofttimes became more known as "brick and mortar" men than as theologians since the need for buildings to provide even minimal spiritual care for the vast numbers of rapidly arriving Catholics as well as that demanded by natural increase made building programs a top priority.

These needs were not only for churches and schools, but in the founding of hospitals, orphanages, and homes for the aged so that these needs of the immigrant could also be addressed and he could find a friendly welcome in the religious atmosphere he had known from his childhood. By 1900 the Church had erected over 825 institutions of private charity, and this did not include all the agencies operating under the influence of the Church.

Perhaps even more of a problem than the recruitment of staff was the internal struggle for the definition of what it means to be a Catholic in the United States. This was not only an ideological concern, but also a matter of ethnic pride; and it was a tension that was to divide the church until well into the twentieth century.

In 1866 there was convened in Baltimore the Second Plenary Council of the Church. High on the agenda were such issues as demonstrating that the Civil War had not disrupted the Roman Church as it had divided most of the Protestant groups and establishing ecclesiastical discipline. Concerning the first issue, the session declared a belief that "the pope speaks with living and infallible authority," thus underscoring the conservative nature of the Church which allows it to rise above the American scene and take its refuge in the chair of St. Peter. Implied in this action was a commitment of obedience to the movements taking place in Rome and culminating during the long pontificate of Pius IX. The Americans were in full sympathy with the pope's action in 1854 in promulgating the dogma of the Immaculate Conception of Mary by which the Church teaches that at the moment of her conception the Virgin Mary was freed from the taint of original sin. This movement intended by the pope as a trial balloon in his effort to insure papal power over the theology and devotion of the Church as he was losing political power over the centuries-old Papal States was widely acclaimed as specifying what had been for centuries a popular feeling in the Church. A decade later, Pius IX came forth with his Syllabus of Errors in which he condemned much of the political theory and attitude toward religious freedom that were integral to the American scene. The pope, while not unaware of the developments in America, was more concerned at the moment with the various understandings of liberalism that were manifesting themselves in Europe, both within as well as without the Church. For the Catholic in America, this papal pronouncement, which was in essence a catalog of prior papal statements, was an embarrassment as from the point of view of the Church it placed him at odds with the Protestant dominated American political and religious scene. The Catholic in America tried to ignore the Roman statement, and for the most part attested his loyalty to American traditions, though his American detractors were not hesitant to bring this matter before his and the public's attention. Also implied in the action taken at Baltimore was support for the trend than being advanced by Rome, which was to achieve culmination in the Spring of 1870 at Vatican Council I with the proclamation of the dogma of papal infallibility. Frequently misunderstood, the doctrine is quite narrow in its scope, but was given a considerably wider latitude by the faithful. Technically what the dogma proclaimed was that when the pope speaks *ex cathedra*, that is, "when in the discharge of the office of pastor and doctor of all Christians, by virtue of his supreme apostolic authority he defines a doctrine regarding faith or morals to be held by the universal Church, by the divine assistance promised to him in blessed Peter, is possessed of that infallibility which the divine Redeemer willed that His Church should be endowed for defining doctrine regarding faith or morals." This clearly implied a universal church under doctrinal and moral obedience to the bishop of Rome. While this set the American Catholic in the context of the universal church under Roman control, it did add fuel to the antagonists of the faith that the Church was just that, and again seen as incompatible with the freedom loving American political and religious scene.

This fear was heightened by such remarks as an article in the *American Catholic Quarterly* in 1877 which dismissed the Declaration of Independence as a flock of vague cliches, and when a few years later a pastoral letter of the bishops of the province of Cincinnati called into question the idea that a people should rule themselves. Then in 1885 in the encyclical letter *Immortale Dei,* the usually diplomatic Pope Leo XIII directly stated the right of the papacy to judge when the affairs of the civil order must yield to the superior authority of the Roman Church, which was further clarified by the official Vatican newspaper, *Osservatore Romano,* in stating that "the Pope is the sovereign of the Church ... he is also the sovereign of every other society and of every other kingdom." Such medieval traditions as these the Roman Church would not officially let go in the political climate of late nineteenth century Europe; but this also pointed out how difficult it is for an Italian pope, hemmed in by past traditions, and involved in contemporary politics, to sensitively address the Catholic population throughout the world. Recognizing the seriousness of the situation, the Third Plenary Council meeting in 1884 had directed the members of the priesthood to refrain from making public statements on political issues, while affirming the separation of church and state.

Before the Second Plenary came to a close it had spoken out on how a disciplined American hierarchy should conduct itself in an overwhelmingly Protestant community. It was more in regard to this action than in the affirmation of loyalty to the Roman tradition, wherein lay the seeds for disagreement within the Catholic community in America.

The term "Americanism" is that which is often used to describe this struggle for identification within the Roman Catholic Church in the United States. The conservative side of the issue was vividly brought to the fore in 1891 when Peter Cahensly, the secretary of the Archangel Raphael Society, a German society organized in 1871 to aid German immigrants, sent a memorial to the pope. The Germans were then the most reluctant to Americanize, and spelled out this trait by requesting that the national groups in America should have their own churches, parochial schools, priests and bishops; or in other words, there should be perpetuated in heterogenous America the ethnic Catholic churches of Europe. The argument advanced was that millions of strongly ethnic Catholics were being lost to the Roman Church. This was a rather radical proposal as the Roman Church had for centuries insisted upon being administered according to geographical units, in fact its whole system of parishes, dioceses, and provinces was predicated on a geographic base so that everyone fell under the jurisdiction of the church authorities established for that area. It is true that there were exceptions to this rule in Europe, but they were the exceptions that helped establish the norm. Implied in this was that the Germans were not satisfied in finding their religious concerns so often in the hands of Irish priests and monks.

The American hierarchy overwhelmingly opposed this proposal, wishing to retain the traditional unity of the Church in its administration, and embracing at times a considerable heterogeneity of the faithful. The papacy acted to uphold the traditional format; yet, separate racial and linguistic congregations also continued to be formed.

A leading spokesman for the other side of this controversy was Thomas Hecker, the founder of the Missionary Society of St. Paul the Apostle, popularly known as the Paulists. His views became more widely known as the result of a biography published shortly after his death, which was a catalyst to once again directly involve the papacy in the American scene. In his concern to bring other Protestants into the Catholic fold, since he was a convert himself, he wished to make Catholicism attractive to persons of Protestant persuasion. He did not wish to detract from papal authority; but he did wish to minimize its presence by stressing independent thinking and personal initiative, two aspects of religious faith common to nearly all American Protestant groups.

This served to pinpoint the differences between leading

members of the American hierarchy. Two prominent leaders were Archbishop Thomas Corrigan of New York and Bishop Bernard McQuaid of Rochester, leaders of the conservative German and Irish factions, who assumed that Catholicism and the American way of life were fundamentally at odds. Hoping for no more than a kind of mutually advantageous truce between two hostile cultures, these men sought to preserve inviolate the traditions that were being clung to so tenaciously by so many of the immigrant masses in the perplexing and so often overpowering American world. The Irish animus of anything Anglo-Saxon was also certainly to be found here as well. A book by the Redemptorist Father Michael Muller entitled: *The Catholic Dogma: Out of the Church There Is No Salvation*, published in 1886, pursued the theme of refuting "those soft, weak, timid, liberalizing Catholics, who labor to explain away all the points of Catholic faith offensive to non-Catholics, and to make it appear there is no question of life and death, or heaven and hell, involved in the differences between us and Protestants."

On the other side stood such men as Archbishop (after 1886, Cardinal) James Gibbons of Baltimore and Archbishop John Ireland of St. Paul. Ireland in a blaze of oratory at the Third Plenary Council declared: "There is no conflict between the Catholic Church and America." He then went on to assert "that the principles of the Church are in thorough harmony with the interests of the Republic." This paean of praise continues with this patriotic pledge to America: "Thou bearest in thy hands the hopes of the human race, thy mission from God is to show to nations that men are capable of highest civil and political liberty.... Believe me, no hearts love them more ardently than Catholic hearts,...and no hands will be lifted up stronger and more willing to defend, in war and peace, thy laws and thy institutions than Catholic hands." Cardinal Gibbons summed up the theological posture of this position in his popular 1876 publication, *The Faith of Our Fathers*. Gibbons insisted that the contemporary

Catholics should emulate the first Roman Catholic Bishop in America, John Carroll, by stating that his aim had been that "the clergy and people—no matter from what country they sprung—should be thoroughly identified with the land in which their lot was cast; that they should study its laws and political constitution and be in harmony with its spirit; in a word, that they should become, as soon as possible, assimilated to the social body in all things pertaining to the common domain of life." Ireland in stressing that the Church in America must be as Catholic as the Church of Rome; "but as far as her garments assume color from the local atmosphere, she must be American. Let no one dare to paint her brow with a foreign taint or pin to her mantle foreign linings."

What was at stake here was not an overt change in dogma as these men did not propose new doctrines, but rather cultural assimilation; yet their opponents were not so sure that this was actually the case. A case in point was the participation of Gibbons and others at the World Parliament of Religions held at Chicago in 1893 in connection with the Columbian Exposition. At the opening session he led the assembly in the Protestant version of the Lord's Prayer. Other Catholic prelates presented papers or presided at general sessions; and while they did so from the motivation that this gathering presented a rare opportunity to present Catholic truth to those outside the fold, their antagonists were greatly disturbed as these actions to them meant a compromising of the faith in their willingness to share the same platform with other religious figures, many of whom did not even claim the name Christian. This conference gave concrete testimony to what had been widely publicized as a result of James Freeman Clark's sympathetic portrayal of *Ten Great Religions*, published in 1871 and going through twenty-one editions in the next fifteen years. This did not deter these Catholic spokesmen from continuing in their efforts to make meaningful contacts, especially with Protestants.

Another bone of contention between the two factions was the decision of the 1884 Plenary Council to establish the Catholic University of America and to locate it in Washington D.C. In 1889 the necessary papal approval was given over the objections of Corrigan, McQuaid and the Jesuits, who all feared that this would lead to a rival center of influence that could be dominated by the "Americanists". With the appointment of Gibbon's friend, Bishop Keane of Richmond, as rector these fears seemed confirmed. However, in 1896 the pope removed Keane from office, a stunning blow to the "Americanists", but a cause of jubilation to the conservatives.

This papal act came about as a result of the sending of Francesco Satolli to the Columbian Exposition bearing with him certain memorabilia of Columbus. His instructions also included an investigation of the turmoil on the American scene and an attempt to mediate the difficulties. Now that the pope had his own representative in America, he was better informed as to what action to take; and upon the recommendation of Satolli, Keane was removed. Another clamp was placed on the church in America when the pope invested Satolli with the office of Apostolic Delegate, that is, his personal representative to assume the leadership of the American Catholic community, rather than creating an American primate, to which privilege Gibbons was the most likely candidate. Then in 1895 Leo XIII issued the encyclical letter *Longinqua Oceani* to the American Catholics, in which, in spite of the praise for the accomplishments of Catholicism in America, he added this note: "it would be very erroneous to draw the conclusion that in America is to be sought the type of the most desirable status of the Church." He further insisted that the Church in America "would bring forth more abundant fruits if, in addition to liberty, she enjoyed the favor of the laws and the patronage of the public authority."

Leo XIII, the diplomatic successor to the uncompromising,

doctrinaire Pius IX, was having second thoughts about his own policies. Being defeated in his diplomatic efforts to regain the papal states lost in the unification of Italy, learning of the infecting of European, especially French, Catholicism by the thoughts of Gibbons and Ireland and a faulty translation of the biography of Hecker, and hearing of the conservative rebuttal that was further raising the tensions in the European Catholic world, Leo decided to speak in such a way as to ameliorate both groups in America and Europe. This he attempted in his letter "Testem Benevolentiae" addressed to Cardinal Gibbons in 1899. In this document the pope declared "that We cannot approve the opinions which some compromise under the head of Americanism.... For it raises the suspicion that there are some among you who conceive of and desire a church in America different from that which is in the rest of the world." Among the doctrines condemned were: (1) that "the Church ought to adapt herself [and]... show some indulgence to modern popular theories and methods;" (2) that "not only some of the rule of life but even some of the deposit of faith from the early church be passed over or softened;" (3) that the "faithful may act more freely in pursuance of his own natural bent and capacity;" and (4) that "the methods which Catholics have followed thus far for recalling those who differ from us is to be abandoned and another resorted to."

Gibbons, Ireland and others coupled their submission with a declaration that "Americanism" was a "phantom heresy" which was not to be found in America, but in Europe, where such ideas were indeed prevalent calling forth a severe papal condemnation in 1907 and the purge of the Church carried out three years later. The conservatives knew that similar ideas were being expressed in America. However, in America the liberal stance was rarely a matter of theology, except in the area of church and state questions, but rather was of a decidedly more practical bend.

The effect of the condemnation of "Americanism" only

accented the prevailingly conservative temper of the largely immigrant and urban American Catholicism. Now whatever bold experimentation there had been gave way to timidity as the Church was still in the throes of meeting immediate religious needs of the ever arriving immigrant groups.

Two other issues also touched the sensitivities of the Catholics in America. One, the question of parochial schools, was to continue as a concern not only within the Roman Church, but frequently to be in the forefront in the political limelight as well. The Roman Catholic leaders correctly perceived that the public school system was not religiously neutral, but in fact had a rather strong Protestant orientation; and as it is an axiom of the Church that the child should be instructed in religion from his earliest years, the 1884 Plenary Council stated that "near each church, where it does not exist, a parochial school is to be erected within two years... unless the bishop, on account of grave difficulties, judge that a postponement be allowed." The directive was strongly worded: "We not only exhort Catholic parents with paternal affection, but we command them with all the authority in our power, to procure a truly Christian education for their dear offspring; to defend them from the dangers of secular education during the whole term of their infancy and childhood; and finally to send them to Catholic and especially parochial schools." Even with the Germans, the most prosperous element in the American Catholic population, strongly committed to this institution, progress was slow; so that the number of parishes so equipped rose from forty percent in 1884 to only forty-four percent in 1892. With the abatement of the internal difficulties by the latter date, there was considerable increase in the parochial school program so that in 1914 over one million pupils were enrolled, primarily in elementary schools as less than seventy-five thousand were attending Roman Catholic high schools. Even on the elementary level a very large proportion of Catholic children were still attending public schools. Yet what had been accomplished was due to the three factors of heavy Catholic concentration in compact urban areas, the sacrificial devotion of the financially strapped Catholic families to nonetheless support the enterprise, combined with the availability of teaching orders to provide at relatively low cost the necessary staffs.

There was dissention in the Church over these schools. Archbishop Ireland praised the work of the public schools and advocated the use of the English language in both church and school. He doubted that the church schools were worth the enormous financial outlay necessary to build and maintain them and appeared also to be convinced that the welfare of the immigrant would be enhanced by a free public education. To seek to please both positions, Ireland tried to work out a scheme for the cooperation of church and state in education that became known as the Faribault Plan. Under this arrangement the Minnesota town took over the parochial schools, paid approved Catholic teachers, and allowed religious education after school hours. This arrangement was in operation only for two years, 1891-1893. There were other similar programs that worked over longer periods of time, and when an American Catholic theologian asserted that the state has the right to educate its citizens and to set academic and other requirements for its schools, the Faribault Plan was submitted to Rome, where it did win the approval of the Congregation de Propaganda Fide. The Church in Rome continued to support such programs, but when the attempt to use tax money for sectarian educational purposes was defeated time and time again the pope finally intervened in favor of a complete system of parochial education, without foregoing the spasmodic demand for some form of public financial support for this endeavor. The conservatives hailed this as a victory, not only for the perpetuation of Catholicism in the United States, but for its preservation in various European cultural forms, a desire many immigrant Catholics wanted to see carried on by their children and grandchildren.

The other issue was the relationship of the Church to the problems of labor. Also here the Church had particular reason to be concerned as so much of its membership potential lay in the laboring class, many of whom were at least nominally Roman Catholic from their European back-ground. Nonetheless the church leadership took a generally very conservative stance, such as Cardinal Gibbons who applauded Carnegie's essay on "Wealth." A year before the devastating strikes of 1877, another archbishop stated that God allows poverty "as the most efficient means of practising some of the most necessary Christian virtues, of charity and alms-giving on the part of the rich, and patience and resignation to His holy will on the part of the poor." There simply were not significant criticisms of the American economic scene or calls for reconstruction of American economic life. This also reflects the position of the papacy, as enunciated by Leo XIII in 1891 in the encyclical *Rerum Novarum* in which, while attacking both socialism and capitalism, he called for the reaffirmation of the medieval guild system which assumed a basically static society with a definite managerial class and labor class, but working together in a harmonious relationship that was for the good of the entire society; all of this under the careful tutelage of the Roman Catholic Church whom God had appointed as the guardian of good order.

As labor unrest mounted with the strikes and subsequent violence, the Church hierarchy took a dim view of the labor unions. Archbishop Bayley of Baltimore stated "no Catholic with any idea of the spirit of his religion will encourage them," and a Catholic paper asserted that the correct solution to economic woes was for the workers to "Pray, Pray, Pray." Then Cardinal Gibbons took hold of the situation by investigating the major labor organization, the Knights of Labor, whose membership was two-thirds Roman Catholic. Receiving assurances from Terence V. Powderly, the Catholic head of the union, that the activities of the organization were lawful, and that its codes of secrecy were no threat to the Church, Gibbons took his findings before the nation's Catholic archbishops. Nine of the eleven agreed that the Knights should not be censored as had already happened in Quebec; but failing to get unanimity, Gibbons himself took the issue to Rome when he went to receive his cardinal's hat. There he stated that a formal condemnation of the Knights would have harmful consequences for the Roman Catholic Church in America. These consequences, he said, would be to alienate the laboring class in America which, as has been noted, was potentially Catholic in great numbers. A condemnation would be seen by many as un-American, a charge the Church should not needlessly bring upon itself; and the Church might drive its own members away if it would not stand by them when they had such great needs. In 1888 Gibbons received a favorable ruling from Rome, that while the labor union would not be approved, neither would it be condemned; it would be tolerated. This was a significant victory for Gibbons as the direction of Rome was clearly in the direction of condemnation of such organizations elsewhere. It was also a victory of those generally associated with the condemned "Americanism" over the conservative forces within the Church. Gibbons then proceeded to give advice to the Knights, admonishing them to avoid the use of strikes and boycotts. Even though the Knights of Labor soon fell by the wayside as an important labor spokesman, this fragile alliance with the Roman Catholic Church opened the door by which Roman Catholic activity did become identified with conservative aspects of labor agitation. The Church did not turn its back on the plight of the urban laborer as did so much of Protestantism, and in so doing helped preserve and increase the loyalty of the industrial masses to the Church. The Catholic laborer thus remained a mainstay of both his union and his church. The capstone of the Church's outreach on behalf of the laborer came in 1917 with the organization of the National Catholic War Council to meet the special needs of World War I. Being made permanent in 1922 by papal action, the organization became known as the National Catholic Welfare Conference. In 1919 Msgr. John A. Ryan prepared a document that was adopted and came to be known as the Bishop's Program of Social Reconstruction, and is somewhat similar to the Social Creed adopted seven years earlier by the Federal Council of Churches. Not calling for a radical reconstruction of American society after the war, it did urge the continuance of the higher wages paid during the war years to many, a reduction of the cost of living so that the real wages would indeed be increased, the continuance of some form of public housing projects, the establishment of a legal minimal wage, social insurance, the right of labor to participate in industrial management, vocational training programs, and the elimination of child labor. Thus as the nation entered into a period of restricted immigration by federal law in the 1920's, the Roman Catholic Church became more vocal in its pronouncements to increase the standard of living for millions of its devoted followers.

Though on a considerably reduced scale, a somewhat similar story initially is that of the growth and development of Judaism during this same era. At the close of the Civil War there were probably somewhat less than a quarter of a million Jews in the United States, but by the opening of World War I this number had grown to nearly three and one half million with almost two million having been European immigrants. Another similarity with the Roman Catholic population is that the Jews were concentrated in the urban centers, the larger the city the heavier the concentration. Jacob Riis reported in 1891 that seventy per cent of the Jewish immigrants remained in New York City, and at the outbreak of World War I approximately one half of the Jews living in the United States still resided there. In 1865 the German Jew was the dominant factor in American Jewish life, but after 1871 the immigration from Germany declined as conditions for Jewish life in that European country markedly improved after the Franco-Prussian War. The shift to eastern European countries as the origin of immigration is seen in the increasing tides of Polish, Romanian and especially Russian Jews entering the United States beginning in the 1880's. This was due in large part to the Russian policy of severe harassment that resulted in a large and prolonged exodus. These Jewish immigrants were very poor and had always been so; and in their homeland had lived almost totally isolated from the surrounding population. Living in a hostile environment they had developed a distinctive and circumscribed life.

The life awaiting these immigrants in "the Promised City" of New York or other major cities was not at all pleasant. Referring to the Jewish ghetto in the slums of New York, Riis reported that "it is said that nowhere in the world are so many people crowded together on a square mile as here." Though they suffered the same consequences of other immigrants, Riis was careful to point out that "the diseases these people suffer from are not due to intemperance or immorality, but to ignorance, want of suitable food, and the foul air in which they live and work." Under the most impoverished conditions the entire family labored long and hard, with the most prominent work resulting in "half of the ready-made clothes that are sold in the big stores, if not a good deal more than half, being made in these tenement rooms."

What was distinctive about the Jews was not so much the various dialects of the Yiddish which they spoke, but that which was found in their religious lives. Here was to be found the determination of these immigrants to preserve the ancient faith that had maintained these peoples for thousands of years. It was readily observed that "when the great Jewish holidays came around every year, the public schools in the district have practically to close up. Of their thousands of pupils scarce a handful come to school." The synagogue and its traditions did play an important role in the lives of these impoverished and persecuted people; and "attached to many of the synagogues, which among the poorest Jews frequently consists of a scantily furnished room in a rear tenement, with a few wooden stools or benches for the congregation, are Talmudic schools that absorb a share of the growing youth."

As determined efforts were made to preserve the Jew in his ancestral faith, there were also definite programs of assimilation to make the old faith meaningful to the Jew living in the developing America. A major step in this process was the spiritual emancipation announced by the Reform rabbis in the Pittsburgh Declaration of 1885. This provided for the rejection of all Mosaic laws concerning ceremonialism that could not be harmonized with contemporary thought. In accenting the progressive nature of Judaism, the *Declaration* asserted: "We consider ourselves no longer a nation but a religious community, and therefore expect neither a return to Palestine, nor a sacrifical worship under the administration of the sons of Aaron, nor the restoration of any of the laws concerning the Jewish state." This document was recognized by most of the synagogues then existing and provided for the increasing disengagement of Judaism from historic normative patterns. Many Jewish congregations adopted the forms of liberal Protestant church worship and practice, even including holding public services on Sunday. This movement for the socially and financially rising Jews was centered in the Union of American Hebrew Congregations formed in 1883, and the Hebrew Union College and Seminary founded two years later and located in Cincinnati, Ohio, both under the leadership of Rabbi Isaac M. Wise.

However, with the tide of immigration developing in the 1880's a strong reaction to this assimilation set in and found an early expression in the establishment of the Jewish Theological Seminary in 1885 in New York. The purpose of the school was to train a religious leadership that was "faithful to Mosaic Law and ancestral tradition." With the coming of Solomon Schechter, Romanian-born scholar, as president, the school assumed an important place in American Judaism; and this was enhanced when Schechter founded in 1913 the

United Synagogue of America, a federation of congregations sympathetic to this understanding of Judaism. The stated aims of Conservative Judaism were:"(1) to assert and establish loyalty to the Torah and its historical exposition; (2) to further the observance of the Sabbath and dietary laws; (3) to preserve in the service the references to Israel's past and hopes for Israel's restoration; and (4) to maintain the traditional character of the liturgy with Hebrew as the language of prayer." Yet there were also accommodations to the American scene as mixed choirs, family pews (instead of seating by sex), organ music, and other decidedly contemporary Christian worship practices. In using some new forms, but keeping the basic content, and interpreting the Jewish writings in the traditional manner, this understanding of the religion sought to directly address the teeming masses in the urban ghettoes.

There were those, especially among the recent immigrants, who could not abide either of these two movements and sought a more rigid preservation of the historic faith in this new land. These were the Orthodox, and though without much financial backing and with a loose organization they kept their faith alive, being aided in doing so by the seemingly endless waves of immigration. In 1898 Henry Mendes gave a stronger organizational bent to this point of view when he organized the Union of Orthodox Jewish Congregations and four years later appeared what was later to be called Yeshiva University to train English speaking Orthodox rabbis.

Differing congregational affiliations and schools for training religious leadership developed as the Jews sought to retain their religion in the form that the individual groups thought appropriate. The number of congregations in New York rose from 270 in 1880 to 1900 by 1916, and though many were small, there is the evidence of the desire to retain the religious tradition. However, the pervasive influence of the public schools sought to Americanize these immigrants, and this influence came to be more dominant than that of the synagogue in forming the character of the succeeding generations. Another possibility for Jewish identification during this era was the promotion of Zionism, but the influence of this movement to reestablish a political Jewish state was primarily after the British issued the Balfour Declaration in 1917 favoring "the establishment in Palestine of a national home for the Jewish people."

In spite of this multiple choice, religious Jews lamented that it was increasingly difficult to retain the generations of Americans born within the orbit of any form of Jewish religion. To be a Jew was increasingly becoming a matter of ethnic identification and not religious; so that the percentage of those who could be expected to identify with Jewish religious institutions and traditions was markedly lower than the percentage of Gentiles identifying with some Christian denomination. At the opening of World War I the increasing inability of Judaism to retain its membership potential did differ widely from the contemporary Roman Catholic efforts.

4

Campaigns for the Soul

Revivalism had made a distinct impact on the American Protestant scene long before the Civil War. The techniques that had been developed by the churches in attempting to reach and revitalize the American people were continued, and new forms were added in the half century following the War. As revivalism had so penetrated the life of most denominations prior to the War, there was to be seen no let up of this distinctive contribution of Protestant Christianity in the decades that followed.

The camp meeting that had begun in the Kentucky wilderness at the opening of the nineteenth century continued in its pattern of being a viable means of instilling religious interest in the first decades of settlement in a particular area. A reminiscence by Olga W. Johnson of life in the northern Rockies in the first decade of the twentieth century included this recollection: "Folk would come in their covered wagons, with a cow tied to the back of the wagon, bring bedding for the family and grub for themselves and others who might be eating with them. Of course everything was very primitive. All the preachers would try to be there as many days as they could stay. It was an occasion to be looked forward to and planned many weeks before and possibly remembered the rest of their life for many were converted." Whether it was in the Great Plains or in the Intermountain West, this form of religious outreach and nurture was an effective instrument in an area still very sparsely settled.

More common was the continued use of what Charles G. Finney had developed and labeled as the Protracted Meeting in the 1820's. This became the most popular form of American revivalism, and involved bringing the revival indoors into the churches of the small towns of America. Here at a relatively slack time in the lives of the people, an evangelist would be engaged to preach a series of stirring sermons on successive evenings. Many congregations so programmed their activity that at least one series was held each year, and for some churches this was the chief arm of membership recruitment. The sermons were not as glowing in their portrayal of hell and then the blessedness of heaven as those delivered out-of-doors by torchlight at the camp meetings; but the approach was now made that night after night in the crowded small churches the case for Jesus could be argued so that after a few nights it would be difficult not to accede to the preacher's claim for the good life to be found in the Christian faith. Attention was centered on the anxious bench, that pew immediately in front of the pulpit, where one who was concerned over his religious life could come and sit, and be the object of the particular effort of the preacher and the prayers of the congregation.

In spite of some denominational aversion to the emotionalism that was suspected as being the motivating force at many of these meetings, and despite the new theological currents that were proclaiming the nurture of the Christian life as if one had never been other than a child of God as the primary function of the church, many mainline Protestant congregations, especially in the rural and small town areas where Protestantism had its strength, longingly looked forward to the annual experience of recruitment and renewal to be provided by the revival.

With the emergence of the industrial and urban post-Civil

War America, there was ushered in a new form of the revival technique, the urban campaign. The desire was now to rekindle the piety of an earlier day with its simple approach to God; and to do this with intense personal dynamics in the mass meeting of a great arena. It was all summed up in the statement of D.L. Moody: "It doesn't matter how you get a man to God provided you get him there." It was still the results that counted.

In the age of the business tycoon and the gigantic corporation stands Dwight L. Moody (1837-1899), a peer among such men and their enterprises; but one not dedicated to the amassing of great numbers of dollars in his bank account, but of securing vast numbers of souls for the kingdom of heaven. Born to a staunch Puritan family that could trace its New England roots back to the 1630's, he exemplified the twin characteristics of such people: being capable of great physical endurance and having a capacity for hard, continuous work. With a love of liberty, a loyalty to conviction, courage in the face of obstacles and sound judgment in organization he became the primary entrepeneur of the massive urban revival campaigns of the last quarter of the nineteenth century. More than any other single individual, Moody determined the religious climate of the country in the immediate post war decades and he stood near the center of almost every agency devised by the churches to implement their task.

His father died when Dwight was four years old, leaving behind, with the birth of twins a month later, a family of nine: seven boys and two girls. The father having made no provision for his sudden death left the family in severe financial straights, but with the help of relatives and the tenacity of the mother, the family was held together, even though the boys hired out on area farms. Dwight, however, became impatient with the restrictions of farm life, and at the age of seventeen left Northfield, Massachusetts, for Boston to make a career for himself. Having only enough money to get to the city, and not being able to immediately find employment, he had to cast himself on the mercy of an uncle who operated a shoe store. Submitting his independent spirit to the uncle's guidance, and promising to attend church and Sunday school regularly, he was taken on as an employee. The uncle soon learned that he had made a good business move in hiring his young nephew. With his keen perception and irrepressible energy, young Moody became a successful salesman. Having no acquaintance with business, he was not to be hemmed in by the ordinary methods of the salesman; and so crying his wares before the door, and actually going out into the street to persuade uninterested passers that they wanted to buy, he became the most productive salesman in the store.

True to his promise, he began attending the Sunday school and worship services of the Mt. Vernon Congregational Church. One day the teacher of the young men's class stopped at the shoe store to talk to Moody about his soul, and in simple language told Moody of Christ's love for him and the love Christ wanted in return. Right there in the back of the store while wrapping shoes, Moody experienced his conversion to Jesus Christ. Years later Moody recalled the immediate effect: "I remember the morning on which I came out of my room after I had first trusted Christ. I thought the old sun shone a good deal brighter than it ever had before—I thought that it was just smiling upon me; and as I walked out upon Boston Common and heard birds singing in the trees I thought they were all singing a song to me. Do you know, I fell in love with the birds. I had never cared for them before. It seemed to me that I was in love with all creation. I had not a bitter feeling against any man, and I was ready to take all men to my heart. If a man has not the love of God shed abroad in his heart, he has never been regenerated." Soon thereafter he sought membership in the Mt. Vernon Church, but for nearly a year was not admitted, as he could not satisfactorily articulate a theological statement of the meaning of his Christian faith. It was not until 1872 that Moody's conversion experience was completely finalized as he experienced such an outpouring of God's spirit in his heart that he could not even speak of it. This was for Moody the baptism of the Holy Spirit, and on the basis of this he entered into his major urban campaigns with full confidence.

In the intervening years Moody went to seek his fortune in the developing city of Chicago. This was in 1856, but in stating that he intended to amass a fortune of $100,000 he did not at the same time neglect his religious interests. He recalled that as soon as the Moody children had begun attending Sunday school in their hometown, they had been commissioned to bring in other students. Dwight and his brother, George, had been aggressive home missionaries in securing recruits for their village Sunday school. Now in Chicago, Moody at the age of nineteen rented a pew in the Plymouth Congregational Church and undertook to fill it every Sunday. He would hail young men on the street corners, visit their boarding houses, or even call them out of saloons to share his pew. For whatever reasons, the individuals so approached came in such numbers that Moody was soon filling four pews every Sunday.

Also important to Moody was the religious revival that swept Chicago and the nation following the panic of 1857. This was not led by any one individual, but was a general religious outpouring that frequently took its form in the noon hour prayer meetings. The initiation of such a religious habit soon became basic to his life-long religious practice, and another tool was added to his arsenal of evangelistic weapons.

His business success in Chicago as a shoe salesman was also phenomenal. He was continually looking for greater opportunities to develop his business ability. Now he would carefully watch the depots and hotel registers for possible customers from neighboring towns, and also took pride in making better and larger sales than his fellow clerks. He soon became a commercial traveller and was well on his way to becoming one of Chicago's successful businessmen while still in his early twenties. In later years it was said of him that in business ability he was a peer of such Chicago businessmen as Cyrus McCormick, George Armour or Marshall Field.

Still it was to his religious work that he devoted his spare time. To occupy his leisure hours on Sunday afternoon he became involved in Sunday school work. He applied as a teacher to a little mission school on North Wells Street, but was told that as they had an over abundance of teachers, he would be accepted only if he developed his own class. This was the kind of challenge that fitted the personality of young Moody, and on the following Sunday he appeared with a class of eighteen little "hoodlums" that he had gathered. With this success, he then became a recruitment agent for other teachers and did not take a class himself. Then in the fall of 1858 he determined to open a new school in another section of the city. Success attended his efforts here as well, and he soon had secured the North Market Hall over one of the large city markets. This Sunday school eventually became one of the largest in the United States with some fifteen hundred students, and became the occasion for the later organization of the Illinois Street Church, which when moved to a new location became the Chicago Avenue Church, popularly known as Moody's Church. Associating with him in this Sunday school were the largest dry-goods merchant in the city, the president of a bank and other leading citizens, giving evidence of the ability of Moody throughout his life to garner the support of the wealthy for his religious undertakings. He also issued stock certificates on the "North Market Sabbath-school Association; capital, $10,000; 40,000 shares at twenty-five cents each." These shares were for the erection of a new building and "for dividends apply at the school each Sabbath." In addition to the classes, Gospel meetings began to be held nightly in a room formerly used for a saloon. It was here that Moody received the practice and training in preaching that were of such value to him in later years. It was also becoming evident to him that this work was not just an avocation, so that in 1860 he gave up his lucrative business career to devote the rest of his life, without salary, to his religious enterprises.

In his Christian work he continued to have little regard for strict conventionalities that did not appeal to his very practical judgment as useful or effective for immediate gain. Then as the success of his evangelistic efforts began to be noticed, Moody was addressed by friends in other cities soliciting his aid in behalf of young men who had wandered to Chicago and become victims of its vices. Moody left no stone unturned in his efforts to satisfy these requests.

When the Civil War came Moody became involved in the United States Christian Commission to bring religious consolation to the soldiers. Visiting in the camps, and going to the battle fronts, but particularly in ministering to the wounded and dying, the impression was indellibly made upon him that it was necessary to urge his hearers to accept immediate salvation; and this was ever afterwards a conspicuous feature of his manner of address. An oft-repeated illustration of this is the incident of how, on one occasion as was his custom, he accosted a young man, apparently just in from the countryside, with the inquiry: "Are you a Christian?" "It's none of your business," was the curt reply. "Yes, it is," was the reassurance. "Then you must be D.L. Moody!" said the stranger.

Another example of the determined, though rather unconventional way, he went about his work seeking out the unchurched in Chicago is related in this story: "No place is too bad, no class to hardened, to be despaired of. He sometimes takes a choir of well-trained children with him to the low drink-saloons to help him attract the drunkards and gamblers to his meetings. On one such occasion...he entered one of these dens with his choir, and said: 'Have a song, gentlemen?' No objection was offered, and the children sang a patriotic song in fine style, exciting great applause. Mr. Moody then started them with a hymn, and went around, while they sang, distributing tracts. When the hymn was over he said: 'We will now have a word of prayer.' 'No!' cried several in alarm, 'no prayer here!' 'Oh, yes, we'll have a word. Quiet for a moment, gentlemen,' and he offered up an earnest petition. Some of the men were touched, and when he invited them to go to his meeting and hear more, about half of them got up and went." In justifying this Moody stated: "We don't make our services interesting enough to get unconverted people to come. We don't expect them to come—we'd be surprised enough if they did. To make them interesting and profitable, ask the question, How can this be done?" His contemporaries said of him that one of the qualities which made him so successful was his open-mindedness in observing surrounding circumstances, his willingness to receive suggestions and his alertness in adopting them when convinced that they would be successful.

Another example is the incident that while attending a convention he took a walk through the city, and "without stopping, Mr. Moody walked into a store on the corner and asked permission to use a large empty box which he saw outside the door. This he rolled to the side of the street, and taking his stand upon it, asked [for] the hymn, 'Am I a soldier of the Cross?' After one or two hymns Mr. Moody began his address. Many workingmen were just then on their way home from the mills, and in a short time a large crowd had gathered.... The crowd stood spellbound at the burning words, and many a tear was brushed away from the eyes of the men as they looked up into the speaker's honest face. After talking about fifteen or twenty minutes he closed with a short prayer and announced that he was going to hold another meeting at the Academy of Music, inviting the crowd to follow him there." With the singing of the well-known hymn "Shall we gather at the river?" the crowd marched down the street and within a few minutes packed the lower floor of the Academy. After speaking to them again, he dismissed them to go to their homes for the evening meal.

Then in 1867, hearing much of the English methods of work, he went abroad to study what was being done there. This and subsequent English visits came to be the proving grounds upon which Moody developed his techniques that made him the most prominent revivalist in the last quarter of the nineteenth century, though he was never formally ordained. The success of his work in England preceded him home, and soon after his arrival he was at work, first in Brooklyn, then Philadelphia and then in New York City. He accepted the invitations to work in these three great cities in the wake of the 1873 financial depression because "Water runs down hill, and the highest hills in America are the great cities. If we can stir them we shall stir the whole country." Here was a note that ran counter the general Protestant thinking of the time; for having been accustomed by its American experience to think of the small town and rural areas as the mainstay of American religious life, Protestant denominations had not yet been able to develop methods to successfully penetrate the large populations now concentrating in the major urban centers. So it was for many that the challenge presented by Moody met with wide response.

The first American campaign was begun in Brooklyn in 1875. Extensive preparations had been made for these meetings, a characteristic of the business-like way Moody went about these urban revivals. Places for the meetings had been provided and a detailed program had been worked out; but more importantly, there was a union of various denominations in holding meetings for prayer and consultation, and the important pledging to one another of a cordial cooperation in the effort of the campaign. This latter feature was high on the list of demands Moody and subsequent major urban revivalists would make before they would agree to come to a city. If any degree of success was to be expected, the wholehearted support of most of the major Protestant churches needed to be guaranteed from the very beginning of the planning. Among the modern business techniques employed by Moody and consistently used by those who have followed him was the committee structure. There was the finance committee headed by wealthy laymen who raised and ex-pended the funds. A major effort was the "Guaranty Fund", which hopefully was raised before the campaign began and was subscribed to by many men of wealth. A major item was the building of the temporary tabernacle or the alterations necessary in an existing hall. Moody himself laid no claim to financial support to avoid the charge of being a charlatan. There was a prayer committee to select a place for the noon prayer meetings and to put the rank and file to work to pray for the success of the venture. A publicity committee was charged with providing handbills and posters and seeing to it that abundant newspaper coverage was given to the planning of the revival as well as reporting the meetings. A home visi-tation committee, a committee for Bible study, another to train ushers and choir, another to handle ticket distribution were among the various committees carefully organized and supervised so that the entire enterprise would run smoothly and efficiently. This underscored the change in Moody's mind that while at one time he thought the raising of Lazarus to be the greatest work ever done on earth, he had come to think that the conversion of the three thousand on the day of Pentecost was more wonderful still.

The pattern almost invariably followed to accomplish this work was that three meetings were held daily, a morning Inspiration Service at 8:00 a.m., a noon prayer meeting, and the main preaching service at 7:00 or 7:30 p.m. There were no meetings on Saturday and on Sundays preaching was at 4:00 and 9:00 p.m. so as not to interfere with local congregational Sunday morning schedules. He also included women's meetings in the afternoon, and meetings for other particular groups from time to time.

In Brooklyn a rink was engaged for a month and chairs for five thousand persons were provided. Then as interest in the services grew, greater efforts were put forth to reach more people by increasing the number of meetings, and overflow meetings and special services in churches and halls augmented the campaign. In Philadelphia a series of meetings was held in the recently abandoned freight depot of the Pennsylvania Railroad, just before it was converted into a store by John Wanamaker. Then it was to New York and the P.T. Barnum Hippodrome. After this came Chicago and Boston. Aside from the years 1881-84 and 1891-92 when he was in England, Moody filled as many engagements as he could from September to May. Some lasted for as much as nearly six months, and most of them were in the leading cities of America. Sometimes he went to smaller cities, arranging a tour including a chain of cities across some important belt of territory, remaining about three days in each place with other evangelists preceding and following him, and leaving the bulk of garnering the harvest and utilizing the spiritual awakening to the local churches.

At a meeting Moody was greatly concerned to establish a high degree of rapport with the huge audience that was nearly always at hand to hear him. To accomplish this there was an intense and spiritual preliminary service of song and prayer, wherein singing by the great massed choir, by quartettes, duets and soloists as well as by the whole assembly never ceased, except for prayer. When the time came for Moody to speak his appearance was thus described by his son: "you see a short, stout-built, square-shouldered man with a bullet-shaped head set close on the shoulders, black eyes that twinkle merrily at times, and a full but not heavy beard and mustache. The face expresses fun, good-humor, and persistence. The coat is closely buttoned, with a bit of stand-up collar seen over it.... As he stands with hand resting on the rail, you are conscious that it is to see, not to be seen. Like an engineer with his hand on the throttle, like a physician with his finger on the patient's pulse, his mind is on the work before him. A quick, soldierly bearing marks every movement."

W. R. Moody goes on to describe his father's speaking: "Headlong talking would better describe it. His voice is rough, pitched on one key, and he speaks straight before him, rarely turning to the sides." In describing a presentation on the Old Testament figure of Jacob, the writer recalls: "But how real he makes the men! How visibly the deceiving, scheming Jacob stands before us! And how pointedly he applies the lessons of the patriarch's life to the men and women before him! His gestures are few but emphatic—the hand flung forcibly forward with palm open, both hands brought down, hammer-like, with closed fists. But the Bible is too much in his hands to allow frequent gestures. He continually refers to it, reads from it, and keeps it open on the stand beside him. His sermon or lecture is little more than exposition of a Bible truth, or a dramatic rendering of a Bible story, with continuous application to his hearers. . . . He ends abruptly, prays briefly, pronounces the benediction, and when you lift your head he is gone."

He was not a pulpit prince in the tradition of Beecher and Brooks, but in his rapid-fire delivery he was essentially an exhorter and teacher. Observers remarked that superficial weaknesses were evident enough, the slips in grammar, the raw colloquial English, and the rough-and-ready expression. Much of this was edited out of the printed sermons, and even in the lengthy extracts published in major newspapers these were eliminated. Those accustomed to the poetic eloquence of the orators and those who looked for refinement in the worship experience were often repelled by a Moody revival.

Though always dressed as a businessman, and going about his presentation in a business man's fashion, the masses in the audience were entrapped by his utter conviction; and through the use of anecdotes from his experience and of those who sat before him, which he couched in a simple, and not sensational style, with a touch of humor and a touch of pathos, he was able to fill most eyes with tears. Thus by sheer persuasiveness he could engage the sympathies of many in the large audiences, and do this without tolerating any of the emotional outbursts that had tended to mark some revivals. So that while worshipping in the rough halls, sitting on wooden chairs, and listening to a man without a pulpit, many learned that costly churches, stained windows, soft cushions, great organs and trained choirs were not necessary to the worship of God. Those of the poor working classes being driven from the mainline Protestant churches of the rich could find religious consolation at a Moody meeting.

This is summed up in Moody's consistent emphasis in centering his attention upon the will. He was sure that it was the person's will that counted, that you simply had to mold, to bend, to break that will, and once having broken it, the remaining barriers fell to the side. If the will is surrendered than the battle is won. It was his intention never to let a meeting go by without issuing the compelling invitation for the sinner to surrender to the will of God. In this he represented what had happened to revivalistic preaching in nineteenth century America. No longer were revivalists publishing accounts of their campaigns as Jonathan Edwards had done in the mid-eighteenth century by describing what had happened in Northampton, Massachusetts, as *A Faithful Narrative of the Surprising Work of God*. Those converted were no longer the elect of God who had become aware of their election through the agency of the Holy Spirit speaking through the verbal proclamation of the Word of God. Instead the accent was on the sinner acknowledging his sin and turning to the loving Father who stood not only waiting for him to return, but as in the parable of the Prodigal Son, was running to greet him on the first indication that the stubborn and evil will of the child had been broken.

Also unlike many of his predecessors, Moody did not try to scare his auditors out of hell. Hell was not a main theme of his teaching; his natural kindness and tenderness made him lean more to love. He proclaimed the gospel of love, that God's mercy was infinite and that no sinner need suffer, if he would repent. He fervently believed in the existence of hell, but he was determined to attract people to God, and accented this, rather than scaring them out of the torment that awaited the unbeliever.

To be precise in his theology was a matter Moody refused to attempt. When a lady came to him and said, "I want to be frank with you, I want you to know that I do not believe in your theology," he answered: "My theology! I didn't know I had any. I wish you would tell me what my theology is." Another time in London a clergyman asked Moody to print his creed before he began his campaign in the English metropolis. Moody responded: "My creed is in print," and when asked "Where?" he answered: "In the fifty-third chapter of Isaiah." Unlike the theologians of the day, he did not attempt to reconcile scientific and religious thought, nor attempt to meet the onslaught of various philosophies upon the Christian faith. Though very conservative in his preaching, he tried to embrace widely varying shades of theological opinion as was evidenced in the persons who were invited to participate in his summer conferences in Northfield, Massachusetts. It was widely recognized that there was nothing novel in the doctrines that he proclaimed. A note in his Bible stated the Three R's:

Ruin by the Fall

Redemption by the Blood

Regeneration by the Spirit

One of his co-workers thus described the thrust of a Moody campaign:

"1. He believes firmly that the Gospel saves sinners when they believe, and he rests on the simple story of a crucified and risen Savior.

2. He expects, when he goes to preach, that souls will be saved, and the result is that God honors his faith.

3. He preaches as if there never was to be another meeting, and as if sinners might never hear the Gospel sound again; these appeals to decide now are most impressive.
4. He gets Christians to work in the after-meetings."

Probably the most characteristic and original feature of Moody's work was the after-meeting in the inquiry-room, which took place after an evangelistic address, and in which the attempt was made to bring individual souls to the all-important immediate decision. Moody insisted that "people are not usually converted under the preaching of the minister. It is in the inquiry meeting that they are most likely to be brought to Christ." "Personal dealing is of the most vital importance" and he deplored that there were so few who were adept at it. "No one can tell how many souls have been lost through lack of following up the preaching of the Gospel by personal work." In giving advice for this phase of the work he carefully concluded that "it is a great mistake, in dealing with inquirers, to tell your own experience." "He doesn't want your experience; he wants one of his own." Moody is insisting that when Christians work with potential converts that they do not try and conform them to their own image. The charge had been laid against revivalists that they tended to condemn all those who did not fit into the exact same mold that had fashioned their lives. With this Moody would have nothing to do. Instead, he said that one should carry a Bible with him to such a meeting and be active in the use of it, as this is the Word of God that addresses the needs of the inquirers. He also encouraged the use of prayer, stating that "sometimes a few minutes in prayer have done more for a man than two hours in talk." Also "when the Spirit of God has led him so far that he is willing to have you pray with him, he is not very far from the Kingdom." Then when the time is right get a man on his knees, but not too soon; and then urge an immediate decision. Moody's advice was also to never tell a man he is converted; rather let the Holy Spirit reveal that to him. Another person can never tell when another is converted; this is an intensely personal moment that only the individual can perceive. A person can then help the new convert in his faith and lead him in the right direction, but the relationship between God and the person is indeed individual. Here individualism, so potent a belief in the American way of life, is once again underscored.

In reviewing the work of that early New York campaign, the New York *Tribune* stated: "the work accomplished this winter by Mr. Moody in this city for private and public morals will live. The drunken have become sober, the vicious virtuous, the worldly and self-seeking unselfish, the ignoble noble, the impure pure, the youth have started with more generous aims, the old have been stirred from grossness. A new hope has lifted up hundreds of human beings, a new consolation has come to the sorrowful, and a better principle has entered the sordid life of the day through the labors of these plain men. Whatever the prejudiced may say against them, the honest-minded and just will not forget their labors of love."

This optimistic note was later shared by a biographer who estimated "in his rage to save souls he traveled more than a million miles, addressed more than a hundred million people, and personally prayed and pleaded with seven hundred and fifty thousand sinners. All in all, it is very probable, as his admirers claim, that he reduced the population of hell by a million souls."[1]

Not all felt this way. There were those who decried the individualism in his approach, insisting that Christianity was a corporate affair and that it was as part of the family of God that one came to the Father and in that context was also nourished by Him. Also those of the contemporary emphasis on social Christianity took issue with his approach. At the time of his death, a Chicago publication, *The New Voice*, stated: "But when a supreme duty appeared; when it was within his power to have spoken the word that would have meant a mighty moral uplift for the national life of the whole

American people; when, as we believe, the call came to him to lead forward for the civic regeneration of the race, he flinched, lacked courage, and turned his back upon the duty." Henry Ward Beecher said of Moody: "He believes that the world is lost, and he is seeking to save from the wreck as many individuals as he can. I believe that this world is to be saved, and I am seeking to bring about the Kingdom of God on this earth." While Moody was sympathetic to human physical suffering, the misery of the soul was so much more important that he could cry: "I have heard of reform, reform, until I am tired and sick of the whole thing. It is regeneration by the power of the Holy Ghost that we need." The accent of Moody was solidly within the mainstream of the Protestant tradition in America; but it did not overflow into the humanitarian reforms that often accompanied this tradition, and which Moody felt were draining religion away from its true course.

There is one major area in which it seems Moody himself was ambivalent, and that was what was the audience he was seeking to address? On one occasion he is remembered for having said: "I would rather wake up a slumbering church than a slumbering world." More explicit was his observation after concluding a New York campaign: "I did not come to New York to reach sinners, but to reach Christians. I wish them to live on a higher plane, to be comforted to the image of Christ." He was conscious that many in his audiences were at least nominally members of Christian congregations, so that the charge that his meetings were more in the realm of gigantic pep rallies for Christians than vehicles for reaching the unchurched had some veracity. This had also happened in London, and on one occasion he burst out: "It's time for Christians to stop coming here and crowding into the best seats. It's time for 'em to go out among these sailors and drunkards and bring them in and give them the best seats." At his early campaign in Philadelphia he requested a large number of people who had been regularly attending the meetings to remain away so that their seats might be occupied by those for whom the meeting was especially designed. The ensuing audience was described as to whom then was able to gain admittance: "Here and there could be seen the bloated faces of bleary-eyed drunkards, glancing wildly around as though the strangeness of the situation was so overpowering that it required a great effort of will to remain; not a few were accompanied by mothers, wives, sisters, or friends, who, having exhausted human means, had determined to lay their burden upon the Lord."

Undoubtedly there were many church members who came to the meetings, but they did indeed bring those with them that were now outside the influence of the Christian faith. They came at a time when Protestant Christianity, though it had made an accommodation to the American way of life, did make an impact on the society at large; and in so doing held before the people an ideal, which while not practiced to any degree by many, was yet a point of identification with the better way of life. Much of Moody's work may be described as seeking to make that identification a personal experience so that whether the individual was a church member or not was not so important, as all Americans needed to be persuaded that there was for each of them a still better way. One student of the Moody campaigns concludes concerning the inquiry room in which Moody placed so much confidence: "For the most part all that happened in the inquiry room was that pious people became more pious."[2]

Contributing significantly to his work was Moody's use of music. To Moody, music had a practical use. He could not himself distinguish one tune from another, just as he could not carry a tune; but he early recognized the impact music had on his audiences. It was not the music of the denominational hymn book that cast this spell on the vast crowds jamming the meeting halls, but the development of a form of musical expression, which became known as the Gospel Song. Before he launched his career as a mass evangelist,

Moody observed of his listeners that if a good singer would "give out 'Rock of Ages, Cleft for Me,' it won't be long before the hats will be coming off, and they will remember how their mothers sung that to them once they were in bed, and the tears will begin to run down their cheeks, and it won't be long before they will want you to read a few verses out of the Bible, and then they will ask you to pray with them, and you will be having a prayer meeting there before you know it."

A major thrust of his work was then begun and continued for the remainder of his career: that of "Singing the Gospel." For some years Moody looked for the right man to assist him in this area of gospel presentation. Attending a YMCA convention in Indianapolis in 1870 he was introduced to Ira D. Sankey (1840-1918), and within a few months the two were linked together so that one was not thought of apart from the other.

The Moody-Sankey revivals popularized a type of music and actually created the label "gospel song." Here were hymn tunes that were easily sung, readily remembered, and which contained verbal expressions emphasizing personal conversion and relationship to God. They were quite related in content and musical composition to the emotional and spiritual environment that characterized the ministry of the evangelists. It was while on their first major tour of England, that being unable to find an appropriate collection of hymns, Sankey put together his first collection of Gospel songs. Then in 1875, combining efforts with another Gospel song writer, *Gospel Hymns and Sacred Songs* appeared, and this was followed by *Gospel Hymns No. 2* in 1876 and continued to *Gospel Hymns No. 6* in 1891. In 1894 the series culminated in *Gospel Hymns Nos. 1-6 Complete*, containing 739 hymns. This was only one of several major Gospel song collections that were being published at this time, containing the works of such hymn writers as Fanny J. Crosby, who, beginning in the early 1850's and continuing until her death in 1915 at the age of ninety five, reputedly wrote nearly eight thousand

Gospel songs. Millions of copies of these song books were sold, and so much were the royalties that the antagonists of the evangelists charged them with conducting revivals just to sell the books. Moody and Sankey were forced to take every precaution to totally remove themselves from any control over these royalties; and in fact while they were dispersed as Moody desired, the money did not end up in the pockets of the two men.

Upon joining Moody in his campaigns, Sankey began the practice of sitting at a low top organ, with which he always accompanied himself, and without ostentation sang his messages into the hearts and consciences of people in a manner that endeared him to thousands. Sankey's voice was a high baritone of exceptional volume, purity and sympathy. Although he had no formal training, he was able to preserve his voice uninjured through long years of hard usage. Using the new texts as well as new music then appearing, as well as writing his own music, he enveloped the crowds in an emotional experience that recalled for many the tenderness of childhood and identified for them the higher form of life, that under such a spell they unhesitatingly recognized as a desirable objective. One of his most famous contributions was his music for the poem "The Ninety and Nine," which he was frequently called upon to sing:

> There were ninety and nine that safely lay
> In the shelter of the fold,
> But one was out on the hills away,
> Far off from the gates of gold—
> Away on the mountains wild and bare,
> Away from the tender Shepherd's care,
> Away from the tender Shepherd's care.
>
> "Lord, Thou hast here Thy ninety and nine;
> Are they not enough for Thee?"
> But the Shepherd made answer: "This of mine
> Has wandered away from me,
> And altho' the road be rough and steep,

I go to the desert to find my sheep,
I go to the desert to find my sheep."

But none of the ransomed ever knew
How deep were the waters crossed;
Nor how dark was the night that the Lord passed thro'
Ere He found His sheep that was lost.
Out in the desert He heard its cry—
Sick and helpless, and ready to die,
Sick and helpless, and ready to die.

"Lord, whence are those blood-drops all the way
That mark out the mountain's track?"
"They were shed for one who had gone astray
Ere the Shepherd could bring him back."
"Lord, whence are Thy hands so rent and torn?"
"They're pierced tonight by many a thorn;
They're pierced tonight by many a thorn."

But all thro' the mountains, thunder riv'n
And up from the rocky steep,
There arose a glad cry to the gate of heav'n
"Rejoice! I have found my sheep!"
And the angels echoed around the throne,
"Rejoice, for the Lord brings back His own!
Rejoice, for the Lord brings back His own."

The Biblical imagery of "The Ninety and Nine" is so obvious; but another that was popular with Sankey was Robert Lowry's "Where Is My Wandering Boy Tonight?" As Moody prepared to speak to an audience in which he hoped there were lots of young men; young men recently arrived in the city to seek their fortune, and who were in a state of suspended animation between a rural or small town past and an uncertain urban future. To these young men, beset with the temptations as well as the uncertainties of the hour, but brought up in many cases on some form of popular American Protestantism, a rapport could indeed be established by having Sankey clearly sing forth with a touching melody these words:

Where is my wand'ring boy tonight
The boy of my tend'rest care,
The boy that was once my joy and light,
The child of my love and prayer?

Once he was pure as morning dew,
As he knelt at his mother's knee;
No face was so bright, no heart more true,
And none was so sweet as he.

O could I see you now, my boy,
As fair as in olden time,
When prattle and smile made a home a joy,
And life was a merry chime.

Go for my wand'ring boy tonight;
Go search for him where you will;
But bring him to me with all his blight,
And tell him I love him still.

Each verse was followed by the refrain (not sung too fast):

O where is my boy tonight?
O where is my boy tonight?
My heart o'er flows, for I love him he knows;
O where is my boy tonight?

Thus, the plaintiff call of the mother at home could be answered by Moody: "Right here in the tabernacle of the Lord, Mother dear." Yet, Moody was careful to note: "it is not mere gush and sentiment this nation wants, so much as it is a revival of downright honesty."

Through the word, spoken or sung, Moody reiterated his own experience, which he saw being repeated countless times in post-Civil War America. The story of young men and women leaving home as he had done, and in so doing leaving a concerned mother behind. Moody remained in frequent correspondence with his mother and after beginning his revival campaigns made his permanent home in his hometown, just a few houses away from his mother. He was devoted to her and could never forget the love she had for her children, including her oldest boy who ran away from home and had no contact with her for years, but who finally returned to be again embraced by his mother's love. This is all reflected in his preaching of Christianity as he proclaimed the message of love to overcome loneliness in the city, as he presented the greatest friend in Jesus Christ in terms reminiscent of the family life of his youth. In this way Moody sought to steel the character of these emigrants to the city so that their lives would not be corroded by their new urban environment.

An editor of *Harper's* noted in January, 1876, "a great multitude of people always magnetizes itself, and the choral singing of a thousand voices is always inspiring." Yet, statistics, notoriously hard to come by in this kind of work and quoted on both sides of the issue as to whether Moody and Sankey were successful or not, seem to suggest that the two men did indeed boost the morale of the regular churchgoers, who were affected by the singing and preaching in the great urban revivals; but they did not reach the masses and did not add appreciably to the numerical growth of the churches. Furthermore his message was directed toward the rural-born American, the farm boy and girl who possessed at least a knowledge of reading, writing and arithmetic, and who were thoroughly imbued with the spirit and methods of the American success ideal. Moody said "I don't see how a man can follow Christ and not be successful." Realizing that he was not reaching the urban masses composed of so many immigrants who did not even speak "good English", Moody, after 1878, varied his approach and at times spent longer periods of time in a city, and conducted his revivals in churches. Though this saved expenses, it was harder to maintain interest and these campaigns tended to lose their nondenominational character. This form of the revival simply did not have the statistical success that it was thought the mass meetings had.

A major shift came when Moody placed more and more emphasis on the Moody Bible Institute in Chicago, started as early as 1866, but which twenty years later was designed to make men and women familiar with aggressive methods of Christian work so that they could act as pastors' assistants, city missionaries, evangelists, Bible readers, superintendents of institutions, and as such be willing to lay their lives alongside of the laboring class and the poor and bring the gospel to bear upon their lives.

Moody and Sankey were only the best known of a host of revivalists and their singing evangelists, some of whom worked under the Moody organization. Regardless of the success these evangelists heralded, there were those who questioned seriously what was happening. One who did so was Charles M. Sheldon. In *In His Steps* he describes a tent evangelist who conducted a summer long campaign in the Rectangle, the slum section of the city of Raymond. In telling of the preaching of the evangelist, Mr. Gray, the beautiful singing of Miss Winslow, Sheldon narrates how Gray stretched out his hand with a gesture of invitation; "and down the two aisles of the tent, broken, sinful creatures, men and women, stumbled toward the platform." Yet, what was the result of these hard won conversions in this part of town, not the middle class areas where Moody tended to conduct his work? Sheldon's answer is: "Gray had finished his work at the Rectangle, and an outward observer going through the place could not have seen any difference in the old conditions although there was an actual change in hundreds of lives. But the saloons, dens, hovels, gambling houses, still ran, overflowing their vileness into the lives of fresh victims to take the place of those rescued by the evangelist. And the Devil recruited his ranks very fast." To the social reconstructionists, the revivals seemed to avoid the significant issues. Indeed Moody did fight the social Christianity emphasis on the fatherhood of God and brotherhood of Man, as he stated: "I want to say very emphatically that I have no sympathy with the doctrine of universal brotherhood and universal fatherhood...Show me a man that will lie and steal and get drunk and ruin a woman—do you tell me that he is my brother? Not a bit of it. He must be born again into the household of faith before he becomes my brother in Christ."

Another similar analysis came from the pen of Walter Rauschenbusch, who, writing in 1907, stated: "Some who have been saved and perhaps reconsecrated a number of times are worth no more to the Kingdom of God than they were before. Some become worse through their revival experience, more self-righteous, more opinionated, more steeped in unrealities and stupid over against the most important things, more devoted to emotions and unresponsive to real duties. We have the highest authority for the fact that men may grow worse by getting religion." The individual uplift of the revivalist often did not last, and Moody would have agreed that this was usually the case if the local congregations had not been able to nurture the new-born faith; but the charge that the revivalist tended to isolate the person's spiritual life from that of his physical and place so much emphasis on the former as to nearly ignore the latter was the avowed intent of the evangelist. He was convinced that after individual regeneration there would follow social regeneration as a natural development.

By the time of Moody's death the leadership in American revivalism had passed to two other men: Samuel Jones (1847-1906), known as the "Moody of the South", and B. Fay Mills (1857-1916). These men marked a significant shift in the emphasis of the revivalist. Instead of preaching that the conversion of individuals was the solitary goal of religion with all other concerns being answered as a natural outcome of the religious experience, these men emphasized the obligation of Christian living in regard to others in the church, in the community, and in the nation. Salvation was the beginning of a new life of activity that was regulated by the Christian conscience. Whereas Moody had emphasized the gospel of love as the Heavenly Father embraced the repentent sinner, these men preached the law of love wherein Christians sought to follow specific guidelines of behavior to bring forth the kingdom of God on earth. The first major revival Jones conducted was in Nashville in 1885, and this set the tone of his work, which was a combination of popular entertainment and civic reform. He saw as his purpose the saving of the nation from the worldliness and sin "which were turning the churches into 'religious crocheting societies' and the social life of the cities into Babylonian debauchery." What he was saying was that the "old time religion" of the pre-Civil War South was not adequate to meet the crying needs of the New South as industrialism was developing in the 1880's. In his preaching the issues became crystal clear, and he defined the enemies of Christianity as those who indulged in, or condoned, dancing, card-playing, gambling, circuses, swearing, theater-going, billiards, baseball, low-cut dresses, society balls, novel reading, social climbing, prostitution, and above all else, drinking alcoholic beverages. Conversion now meant a change in moral conduct, a resolution to "quit your meanness" and fight for decency; and this was to be accomplished by encouraging paternalistic charity of the traditional type that had been so much a part of the American scene in the nineteenth century, and to impose the moral code of rural Georgia upon everyone whether he wanted it or not.

While Jones was seeking to accommodate revivalism with its accent on individualism to the late nineteenth century American scene, B. Fay Mills "was one of the first and perhaps the only professional revivalist ever to break with the emphasis upon individual reform and to preach primarily a doctrine of social responsibility and social action."[3] Thus the revival technique was used to proclaim the doctrines of the social gospel, and the message came to include that the business of the church was to bring about better care for the poor and to be concerned about the physical welfare of all cities and citizens, including better roads, cheaper heat, light, transportation, and also pure water. Then in 1899 he abandoned evangelism entirely and became the pastor of the First Unitarian Church in Oakland, California, causing his opponents to smile at what they had suspected all along and to cast more suspicion on the theological vagaries of the social gospel.

As the twentieth century opened professional revivalism was clearly aligned with the conservative elements in religion as well as politics and business. As one astute student of the phenomenon of revivalism states: "Evangelists tried to end the growing cleavage between the churches and those outside the churches by utilizing revivalism to elicit or compel conformity to an increasingly narrow pattern of thought and action."[4] This thrust was encapsulated by Warren A. Chandler, a bishop of the Southern Methodist Church. In a book entitled: *Great Revivals and the Great Republic*, published in 1904, he demanded "that the next great awakening be a call to arms, a massive campaign of Christian warfare designed to drive the enemies of evangelical religion to unconditional surrender." This campaign was an association of the popular revivalistic religion with Anglo-Saxon racism and American jingoism, so that conversion became a matter of loyalty to a set of vague Anglo-Saxon and American ideals. The revivalists who constantly reiterated these concepts into the mid-1920's reduced revivalism to ritualistic mass commitments to a social conformity which was identified as the American way of life, at a time when many Americans, still unsettled by industrialism, with its concommitant urban centers populated by the new immigration, were confused as to what the American way really was. There was a recognized dichotomy between rural traditions and urban realities, though there was often a longing to retain rural values in an urban setting.

Expressive of this was J. Wilbur Chapman (1857-1918) and his chorister, Charles Alexander, and from 1904 until his death he practiced a method known as the Chapman Simultaneous Evangelistic Campaign. This consisted of dividing a city into a number of districts, each of which was to conduct a revival simultaneously with every other district. While the two leaders conducted meetings in a large centrally located auditorium, pairs of evangelists and choristers conducted their revivals in churches, theaters and halls throughout the other districts and even in the suburbs. Using this device first introduced by Mills and other devices developed by Moody and refined by others, this method of approaching an entire city at once seemed the most efficient method of campaign yet developed. Personally he was one of the few professional evangelists who did not make much use of aggressive, fiery pulpit techniques. His tone was usually pleading and friendly. He took it for granted that his audiences believed in the popular Protestant doctrine and middle-class virtues. His call to conversion commonly took the form of asking all those to stand who were willing to "get in line with every decent man who is trying to make this city better." His sermons consisted of numerous sentimental stories strung upon some theme which had as its climax an appeal to the best in man, or to the love of home, mother or country. Yet, beginning in 1909 his method slowly went out of favor.

In the second decade of the twentieth century the American scene increased its tempo of life. The most popular year for the circus, so often condemned by the revivalists, was 1910, and also in that year ten thousand movie houses had weekly audiences of ten million Americans; all of this was symptomatic that now to attract the masses to evangelistic crusades real showmanship was also needed. No better illustration of this change is to be seen than in the career of William A. (Billy) Sunday (1862-1935). Born of pioneer parents near Ames, Iowa, his mother became a Civil War widow when he was only a month old. While she tried to keep the family of three sons together, she was unable to do so, and Billy finally came under the care of orphanages. Soon he was on his own, and in his own words: "A hayseed of the hay-seeds." At the age of twenty he was observed playing base-ball by the leader of the Chicago "White Stockings," which led to a brilliant career in professional ball that lasted for eight years. In the meantime he had been converted at the Pacific Garden Rescue Mission in Chicago in 1887, when, after being enticed by the street musicians, he accepted the invitation to visit the mission and continued to go back. What caused his conversion was a rekindling of the memories of his earliest childhood at home, and it was finalized in his pursuit of Miss Helen Thompson, whose Presbyterian minis-ter father would not think of letting his daughter be courted by a nonchurch-attending baseball player. Sunday became active in a church and soon married Miss Thompson. Four years after his conversion he gave up his lucrative baseball career for a position with the Chicago YMCA that was at times as much as six months behind in paying his meager salary. He was not the physical director, but was rather engaged in evangelism. Soon he became an associate of J. Wilbur Chapman, becoming his advance man. Then in 1895 Chapman temporarily withdrew from the work and Sunday was left without employment; but soon an invitation came to conduct a revival in the small town of Garner, Iowa. For the next ten years Sunday labored in the small towns of the corn belt, and during the ten years prior to America's entry into World War I he tantalized their city cousins in many of America's major metropolitan centers.

He soon developed a style that emphasized slangy humor and florid rhetoric. Concerning this humor he would say: "I'm almost afraid to say anything to wrinkle some of your faces and make some of you people laugh. I am afraid I would be arrested for breaking antique bric-a-brac." Though the people were not accustomed to laughing during the preaching of the Gospel, they were accustomed to the rapid-fire of words with which Sunday sprayed them. His biogra-pher describes his speech: "His words smack of the street corners, the shop, the athletic field, the crowd of men. That this speech is loose, extravagant and undignified may be freely granted; but it is understandable."[5] He goes on to comment: "Any kind of a fair play that will get the runners to the home plate is good baseball; and any speech that will puncture the shell of human nature's complacency and indif‐ ference to religion is good preaching." He then admits: Sunday has "gone the limit in popularized speech." One of his favorite objects to attack was the saloon keeper, and in one breath he could roar out about "those damnable, in‐ famous, vile, rotten, black-hearted, white-livered, beetle‐ browed, hog-jawed, weasel-eyed, good-for-nothing, dirty imps of hell and damnation..." and then grin with the round of applause that rose from the crowd. His sensationalism was not just limited to the language style that he would use as a preacher of the gospel; it was also seen in the clothes that he wore. He was a colorful dresser and one reporter noted: "Sunday grew so lurid that he shed first his collar, than his coat, and as he closed his sermon, proceeded to put on his raiment with the nonchalance of a man talking to an intimate friend in his boudoir." When these factors were combined with his athletic ability, the audience was in for a show. When Sunday attacked dancing, a newspaper headlined: "Theater, Cards, Dance Held as Works of Devil; Sunday in Talk of Amusements Lambasts and Mimics While Audience Shrieks" and the story then proceeded: "While the audience shrieked with laughter and clapped their hands till the rafters rang, Billy Sunday, the mimic, last evening shimmied, belly‐ wiggled, bunny hugged, tangoed and high stepped across the platform in imitation of the way the modern 'hotbeds of immorality' are danced...." In his denunciation of tobacco, Sunday stated: "I don't say a man can't be a Christian and use tobacco. But I say he'd be a lot better one if he didn't use it. On the level, don't you respect me more because I can come up here without—he seized a pitcher of water from be‐ neath the pulpit and washed out his mouth, drenching the carpet of the platform with the supposedly polluted residue." So it went with Sunday pounding the pulpit, standing on a chair, swinging a chair over his head, smashing a chair on the pulpit, sliding home "safe for Jesus" across the platform, jumping, falling, staggering, whirling, and even doing hand springs. This was muscular Christianity; the sentimentality of Moody simply was not here.

Observers of the Sunday revivals did note that during the first week of his meetings he puts on the best vaudeville show to be found in America, but they also noted that as the campaign progressed he toned down considerably, and especially on Sundays became "as correctly conventional as an Episcopal rector or a Presbyterian College president."

It was after this first week that he invited his auditors to "hit the saw-dust trail," when at the conclusion of the meeting the congregation was urged to come before the assemblage and shake hands with Billy. What a sight it was to see hundreds of people, of all walks of life, surging forward with arms outstretched to grasp the hand of the perspiring evangelist. All of this took place at a plain board platform, about six feet high and fifteen feet long, covered by a carpet. The only furniture was a second-hand walnut pulpit, directly under a huge sounding board, and one plain wooden chair. However, this was placed in a temporary tabernacle especially built for the campaign. This was a distinctive feature of a Sunday revival. The building helped unite the community in preparation as did the extensive committee work that Sunday borrowed from his predecessors. Sunday insisted on a unity of support from the Protestant churches in the city, even to the extent of closing all churches on Sunday so that all Christian attention was centered at the rough, wooden tabernacle. In this simple building all the seats were on the main floor and that floor was covered with sawdust so that when people "hit the sawdust trail" to shake hands with Billy there would be very little sound. It was Sunday's intention that this rude structure be paid for by popular subscription before he arrived for the campaign. If this was not possible he then received offerings until the bills had been paid. Then there were no more offerings until the last day when a single collection was taken and given in total to Sunday. This was his only "salary" for the campaign, thus seeking to avoid the criticism that he was doing this work for the money. These final day "love offerings" soon came to be quite generous, amounting to nearly one million dollars by 1917.

With the enormous attendances, the reputed number of conversions and the outpouring of dollars to Sunday, it was admitted that he told his audiences what they wanted to hear. His biographer states: "Nobody hears anything new from him.... Temperamentally a conservative, Sunday has taken the truth taught him by his earliest teachers and has adapted and paraphrased and modernized it. In the crucible of his intense personality this truth has become Sundayized." Preaching the same simple evangelicalism that Moody did, he nonetheless reduced theology to the simple choice of heaven or hell: "You are going to live forever in heaven or you are going to live forever in hell. There's no other place— just the two. It is for you to decide. It's up to you, and you must decide now." With Sunday the Gospel also included an aversion to the usual forms of amusements such as dancing, card playing, theater going, and, of course, drinking "booze"; along with condemnations of the unpatriotic Huns, Bolsheviks and Roman Catholics. Once the sinner came down the aisle, shook his hand and signed a decision card he was given a pamphlet which included this statement: "A Christian is any man, woman or child who comes to God as a lost sinner, accepts the Lord Jesus Christ as their personal Savior, surrenders to Him as their Lord and Master, confesses Him as such before the world, and strives to please Him in everything day by day." If one agreed to this, then to make a success of his Christian life the following seven guidelines were given: (1) Study the Bible, (2) Pray much, (3) Win someone for Christ, (4) Shun evil companions, (5) Join some church, (6) Give to the support of the Lord's work, and (7) Do not become discouraged.

Between 1896 and 1906 he conducted one hundred campaigns, ninety of them in cities of less than 10,000 population. Rather reliable statistics point out that in nearly one-third of these campaigns twenty per cent of the population was converted and that a high percentage of these did in fact join local congregations. Though in the next decade the percentage dropped in his work in the major cities, it was justifiable for the New York *Times* to state in its obituary notice: "the greatest high pressure and mass conversion Christian evangel that America or the world has known."

Because he produced tangible results many ministers, and particularly those in the large cities, who may not have agreed with his theology or his flamboyance, invited him to evangelize their communities. Many of the urban congregations were indeed suffering, often not being able to financially survive as their congregations moved away and not being able to gather in the new neighbors.

Part of Sunday's success were new methods of efficiency that were added to the established revival methods. The heart of this was "the Sunday party", a group of more than twenty experts, each of whom specialized in some particular facet of the campaign and who was responsible for directing that part of the work. One of these, in addition to his wife who was the business expert, was Homer A. Rodeheaver (1880-1955), the choir leader, soloist, trombonist, and expert master of ceremonies from 1909 to 1931. Among his compositions was "Brighten the Corner Where You Are," which became the theme song of Sunday's tabernacle campaigns. In defending the gospel song, Rodeheaver wrote: "The gospel song is a declaration of God's plan of salvation and his promises, addressed to the people. We can bring you thousands of illustrations of individuals whose lives have actually been changed by the message of the gospel song, and who

have become assets in their communities where they were lia-
bilities before. These songs are not written for prayer meetings, but to challenge the attention of people on the outside
who have not been interested in any form of church work or
worship. If critics knew how some of these songs were loved
by many people, they would never refer to the 'saccarine
talents' of great and good men who have blessed the world
with their songs." Like Sankey, "Rody" published gospel
songs; but he also moved into the phonograph record business
thus further spreading the revival influence. Another feature
widely used by Sunday was the delegation system, whereby
groups of persons from the various schools, trades, profes-
sions, organizations and communities attended tabernacle
meetings in a body. This technique allowed Sunday to reach
the various strata of the cities, and also gave variety and
publicity to the meetings. This was enhanced by his
continuing the practice of other revivalists in augmenting the
tabernacle meetings with meetings in factories, plants, stores,
and even in private homes.

It was also Sunday's experience that the people he attracted
and converted were in a vast majority of cases the middle-
class Americans whose ideals he was enunciating. Sunday
felt that his most successful campaign was the Philadelphia
revival of 1915 followed soon after by another successful
revival in New York; but then the interest of the nation
became increasingly centered in the war in Europe, and after
the Armistice was signed America turned to still other interests and the influence of Sunday steadily declined. His
playing down the necessity for any personal crisis experience
did equate salvation with decency, patriotism, and manli-
ness, and while this did attract vast numbers for the first
twenty years of his career as an evangelist, it proved less and
less satisfactory for the last twenty years of his work.

Sunday was not alone in his style or in his experience. In
1911 there were some six hundred and fifty active evangelists
on the American scene joined by nearly twice that number

engaged in part-time evangelistic work. Between 1912 and 1918 they staged at least thirty-five thousand revivals. This was the heyday of mass revivalism in the trappings of vaudeville, religion being presented in the forms that the entertainment media were rapidly developing. Like Sunday, those seeking to work in the urban centers found the field not so inviting after the war; but this did not mean that in many areas of rural and small town America there was not a field "white unto the harvest," yet not so many reapers were needed.

As the United States entered World War I, an analysis of revivalism would have to include that thousands, and perhaps millions, had been rejuvenated in their Christian faith by the numerous revivalists at work. There were also significant numbers, how many it is utterly impossible to tell, who were brought to the Christian faith by these same evangelists. In 1917 the social gospel advocate, Walter Rauschenbusch, could say: "To one whose memories run back twenty or thirty years, to Moody's time, the methods now used by some evangelists seen calculated to produce skin-deep changes. Things have slimmed down to signing a card, shaking hands, or being introduced to the evangelist. We used to pass through some deep soil ploughing by comparison." Even the efforts of the earlier evangelists have come under the critical eye, and as it has been pointed out, revivalism "failed to reach the masses; it failed to halt the spread of secularism; it failed to rejuvenate the spirit of the churches, to reestablish the influence of the clergy, to defeat the heresies of modernism, to evangelize the world, and to stem the tide of science worship."[6] Perhaps its greatest failure was that it could not stop the march of time and could not reestablish in the minds of increasingly urban Americans the nineteenth century small town code of beliefs and behavior which was seen as integral to its message.

5

Westward Ho!

The Nineteenth Century has been described as "The Great Century" in the history of modern Christianity when the emphasis is being placed on the vast geographical expansion of the faith. This is also true on the American scene as prior to the Civil War various Christian groups effectively spread across the Ohio and Mississippi River Valleys. Then in the half century following this conflict the denominations pursued the miners, cattlemen and homesteaders to the Pacific Coast, the Great Plains and, as the myth of the "Great American Desert" was exploded, to the Intermountain West.

The expansion of Christianity into trans-Appalachia had been beset with many problems, but most of these had been significantly overcome in the dotting of the forested and grassy plains with enduring congregations, and this was documented in the influence that Christianity, and particularly its Protestant expressions, had made in the shaping of American life by the third quarter of the century. It was to be a different story, however, as Christian forces marshaled their strength for the drive beyond the Missouri River. The East and Midwest with their relatively established agricultural patterns were now moving in the direction of industrialism and its concommitant urbanism, while the South was still seeking to recover from the ravages of the recent civil strife; these were the challenges that occupied denominational thinking. Missions patterns had been set, and the denominations assumed that the successes of the past could be repeated all the way to the Pacific; so it was very difficult for these denominations to realize that the New West was not like the Old West, and then to respond creatively to the realities of these frontiers.

Horace Bushnell had concretized the feelings of many in the East with regard to the Old West in his essay in 1847 entitled: *Barbarism the First Danger*. In this he stated that those who went to the frontier were often the dispossessed and discontent and that in the unsettled areas of the vast frontier the worst side of their character easily came forth so that it was necessary for the good of the American society as well as the Christian church that the civilizing as well as strictly religious forces of the Protestant churches be quickly brought to bear in the new areas of settlement. So now, too, as the westward progress of the line of settlement moved jaggedly onward it was still necessary that these same forces bring the presumed Christian culture to bear in the roaring mining camps, among the roving cowboys, as well as to the homesteaders who were more likely to appreciate the familiar patterns of life back East. At least such a challenge was underscored in Josiah Strong's popular tract entitled *Our Country*, published in 1885 by the American Home Missionary Society, as he made the claim: "The West is today an infant, but shall one day be a giant, in each of whose limbs shall unite the strength of many nations."

Among the major problems presented by the post-Civil War New West was the extractive nature of the industries that developed. This was true whether the local situation was the removing of precious ores or copper, the destruction of native grasses by overgrazing, or the denuding of the soil in an attempt to produce large yields of grain. The concern was for immediate gain, and provisions were not made for the possibility of exhausting the resources which were making the present production possible. Soon placer mining gave out in a particular location and the individual miner was forced to move on, or to become an employee of an Eastern mining corporation if a mechanized mining procedure became feasible, and often even this did not last long. The roving cowboy was the hired hand of the large livestock company which soon became a settled and diversified operation as the open range was fenced. The homesteader's experience was a little different, though he was frequently forced out by drought with his land becoming part of a larger ranch. If the lure of the West had included individual freedom and prosperity, great were the disappointments for many. This was evidenced in the high rate of mobility, which while not at all unusual on the American scene was more pronounced in the New West than in the regions to the East. Eastern denominational executives could not understand why it was so hard to maintain a congregation once begun, for they simply could not understand the lack of community stability, or the sparseness of the local financial resources for sustaining congregational life.

Soon it became vital to the work of the Christian faith in this area that the clergy, and, to a significant degree, the finances be provided by the national denominational bodies. Most of the clergymen who came did so under denominational appointment and with partial if not complete financial support from the East. Much of the success or failure of the churches in individual communities hinged on the personality of the minister. Many were young, inexperienced graduates from the seminaries, who came to the New West ill-prepared to face the different cultural environment; and unfortunately, the adjustment proved too difficult for many of them. Others came with the intention of staying only a short time, and then being promoted to a more desirable position in the East; and some came thinking that anyone could succeed in the West. The result of this was often nearly disastrous, and brought about a clergy mobility that was so serious that the work was greatly hindered. What caused this, basically, was that men trained and experienced in a cultural pattern where the church was a distinct part of society, were not able to participate constructively in a society where the personal element of Christianity had first to be established, and then upon this foundation could a place for the institution of the church be effected.

In the first half of the nineteenth century denominational expansion in the Ohio-Mississippi Valley tended to be governed by one or the other of two basic outlooks. On the one hand there were the paternalistic denominations like the Episcopal, Congregational and frequently Presbyterian churches so prominent in the colonial period and now joined by the later large immigrant Roman Catholic and Lutheran groups that approached the frontier as an area where their own children must be sought out and the blessings of particular cultural and religious backgrounds be strengthened or re-established among them. On the other hand there were the Methodists, Baptists, Christians (Disciples of Christ), and sometimes the Presbyterians who saw in the virgin forests and plains the golden opportunity to shed the undesirable cultural accretions of past centuries and to establish once again apostolic Christianity seeking guidance only from the Holy Scriptures as interpreted by the power of the Holy Spirit.

Implementing these attitudes were differing ministerial methodologies. For the paternalistic denominations the emphasis was upon a formally educated clergy who sought to locate permanently in a community after the place had been identified by a roving missionary who had ascertained the need in that area. It was the clergyman's duty not only to preach the Gospel as that denomination understood it, but to seek to bring to bear the cultural patterns that had nurtured that understanding elsewhere. Another methodology was expressed by the Methodists, who in their intense desire to spread Scriptural holiness over the entire land, established an elaborate network of circuit riders who usually preceded the settling of local preachers in an area so that with infrequent preaching at any given point a large area nevertheless heard the presentation of the Methodist understanding of Christianity. This highly disciplined army of young men soon made the Methodist Church the largest denomination in the United States to be eclipsed in the middle of the century by the immigrant Roman Catholic Church. More prominent in the South were the Baptist farmer-preachers, who pursued one vocation six days a week and the other on Sunday, and the Christians (Disciples of Christ) who looked upon church expansion as a local congregational matter rather than a national denominational concern.

These patterns were somewhat revised in the post-Civil War New West. The paternalistic denominations continued in their established manner, with a more aggressive pattern having been developed by the Episcopal Church which came to insist that the national denomination was at the same time a national missionary society and that the two could not be separated. The result was a church that had been so prominent in the colonial period again came to the forefront in the New West in the latter half of the nineteenth century. The Methodist's successful circuit system fared rather well even in the enormous distances of the New West, but the more Southern based denominations, by now also relying on national denominational resources, did not play the role in this West that they had in previous frontiers. Most denominations practiced a pattern of conservative expansionism, whereby the concern was more with adequate service to the places occupied rather than the number of places reached. Since greater and greater reliance was placed on national denominational support, the mission of the denominations was affected not only by local financial support but by the national financial situation so that national economic depressions played a larger and larger role in denominational expansion and retention of work begun. Denominational policies of retrenchment were not uncommon.

In addition to the work of the clergy there were other important ministerial arms. Chief among these were the Protestant Sunday schools. Often begun as union schools, it was the determination that these soon be made into strictly denominational expressions for the purpose of leading to churches that could receive national support. Many were the congregations that were begun as Sunday schools. Some denominations, such as the Episcopal and Lutheran tended not to use the Sunday school as a congregational starter or expansionist tool, but limited the Sunday school to the other generally accepted function of being a local congregational nurturing agent. Another tool of the churches was the state periodical, composed of the itinerarys of denominational officials and evangelists, devotional material, accounts of regional developments as well as national and world-wide events in the denomination and the church at large. The periodicals were sent on a subscription basis to members willing to pay in an attempt to establish a denominational sense of community and were also sent free to potential members. Another very prominent feature of Protestantism in the New West, as has been noted was also true in the rest of the country, was the use of the revival technique in several forms. In actuality, the history of revivalism in America was telescoped in the New West of the latter part of the nineteenth and early twentieth centuries, and was relied upon very heavily by most Protestant denominations for the dual purpose of recruitment and reactivation. So it was that policies and methodologies painstakingly developed in the Ohio and Mississippi River Valleys were continued as the various Christian churches sought to penetrate and influence this vast new frontier.

With the discovery of gold in California and the immediate rush of the 49'ers, the American Mountain West entered upon an era of boom and bust in the mining camps. The Rev. Jonathan Blanchard, on an exploratory trip for the American Missionary Association in 1864, wrote from the Rocky

Mountains one year after the discovery of gold at Alder Gulch: "It would seem as if God had placed the gold in such centers of physical desolation to show how small an agency God has in making men happy." To this man from the grassy plains of Illinois, this was beyond comprehension; but a few months earlier, the Rev. A.M. Hough had come to this camp, called Virginia City, to establish the work of the Methodist Church, and he portrayed the lively scene in a diary entry: "Here is a city of 10,000 inhabitants, and not a frame or plastered house in it, but consisting of tents, 'dugouts' and log cabins, mostly with dirt floors and no floors. But every place that would shelter a head or furnish a man room to sleep is occupied." Commenting further on the difficulty one encountered when trying to rent any type of accommodation, he concluded his observation by saying: "It seems like an overcrowded beehive." What kind of people were there that Hough hoped to reach with the Gospel? There were strong and experienced miners who came from the gold rushes in California and Colorado, and even from the gold fields across the oceans; there were renegades fleeing from both sides in the Civil War; and there were adventurous tenderfeet from all walks of life in the East. It has been noted that this polyglot condition prevailed even in the later years of mining when railroad transportation made it possible for men of less strength of character to go there who might well be taking Bret Harte stories for their standard and pretending to be what they were not with often disastrous results.

The image by which gold mining camps were known back East was enhanced by such a description of Virginia City that appeared in the *Montana Post* on November 10, 1866:

> The heart of the town is within a hundred yards of the diggings. In flush times, it was a crowd of people, and a whirl of business. Streets were thronged, stores choked with a stream of commerce, sidewalks monopolized by irrepressible auctioneers, hoarsely crying horses, oxen, mules, wagons, and household goods. Drinking saloons,

whose name was legion, were densely crowded. Theaters, which always spring up in mining regions, were
closely packed. At the hotels, beds were hardly obtain-
able, for love or money. Gambling-halls were musical
with clinking coin and shining with yellow gold. Hurdy-
Gurdy houses, with dancing girls, music and long bars,
where whiskey was sold at fifty cents a drink and cham-
pagne at $12 per bottle, were filled with visitors, ranging
from judges to blacklegs, in every costume from broad-
cloth to buckskin. And all of this, in a town less than
one year old, in the heart of the Rocky Mountains, a
thousand miles from everywhere!

The observation suggests that conditions had already
changed, for within a year of the discovery of gold at Alder
Gulch the population had fallen precipitously as the rush was
to the new "diggings" on Last Chance Gulch. The newspaper
then reported: "The American miner is a migratory animal,
who will always leave five dollars per day for the possibility
of twenty, especially when the new diggings are very remote
and inaccessible." To many this all sounded exciting, but to
the people concerned with the possibility of Christian work
in these new places such a description left them perplexed as
to what to do to thwart the advance of barbarism. Episcopal
Missionary Bishop Daniel S. Tuttle helped answer this concern by pointing out that not all miners were wild young
bachelors, but that "in Virginia [City] I find many Christian
women of culture and refinement, sensible men, and earnest
men, and good men, willing to work and give, and help for
the establishment and sustentation of Christianity among
them, homes with home comforts; children, many needing to
be trained for Christ, and to be saved in Christ." This statement published in an article in the national denominational
missionary journal, *Spirit of Missions*, four years after the
discovery of gold there underlined the perception that denominational work begun had a chance of enduring, provided, of course, that the mining continued. The situation in

Virginia City was that after seven years of settlement, only one church remained, and there had never been more than two churches at any one time. In fact, very few ever affiliated with a church. The impact of Christianity on this boisterous and very fluid mining camp had seemingly been very slight. All was not in vain, however. Underscoring a positive note was the first superintendent of the Methodist Church in Montana, A.M. Hough, who stated in his diary after four years of work between 1864 and 1868: "During my stay in Montana, I visited nearly all its settlements and mining camps, traveling on horse or muleback, sometimes with a wagon and sometimes by public conveyance, but always carrying my bedding with me. I preached the first sermons in most of the places, sometimes in saloons or private cabins, and often on the streets; but never had a meeting disturbed, and was never treated with anything but kindness and consideration." To provide a balanced picture is the observation made by Cornelius Hedges, a prominent early resident at Helena on Last Chance Gulch: "for the first 10 years, roughly estimated, Helena was chiefly a mining camp, resembling the New Jerusalem only in one respect, that its streets were paved with gold, a misfortune in our case, for this paving was torn up and run through sluice boxes." Nonetheless, Helena was to endure as it became the permanent capitol of the territory and later the state.

It was to raw, new communities like these that the denominations sent their missionaries to proclaim the Gospel. Though the population was very transient, there were those who would listen to the preacher and those who would also support his work; and as long as the community lasted denominationally supported congregations did have a chance to endure, though at any one time the impression being made seemed very slight indeed.

Following the Civil War the long established cattle trade of the Southwest was greatly enlarged by the extension of the railroads into the Great Plains. It now became feasible for

Texas cattle to be driven north to the new rail terminals to be shipped to the meat-hungry cities of the North. Now as the cow town came into American history so did the image of the cowboy quickly come to prominence. Following the establishment of the shipping center at Abilene, Kansas, in 1867, the roving cowboy moved along the rapidly developing trails, and it was not long before the cattle were being driven beyond Abilene unto the Northern Plains to feast on the abundant native grasses as it was learned that cattle could survive northern winters on the open Plains. This led to the establishment of more cow towns along northern railroads pushing ever westward unto the Plains. In 1880 Granville Stuart took the first herd onto one of the grassy ranges of the Northern Plains. He described this country at that time as practically uninhabited: "One could travel for miles without seeing so much as a trapper's bivouac. Thousands of buffalo darkened the rolling plains. There were deer, antelope, elk, wolves, and coyotes on every hill and in every ravine and thicket." Then he described the same area as it appeared only three years later: "There was not one buffalo remaining on the range and the antelope, elk and deer were indeed scarce. In 1880 no one heard tell of a cowboy...but in the fall of 1883 there were six hundred thousand head of cattle on the range. The cowboy, with leather chaps, wide hats, gay handkerchiefs, clanking silver spurs and skin-fitting high-heeled boots was no longer a novelty but had become an institution." Here was a new frontier rapidly being filled, and what were the chances for a Christian presence? The cowboy proved to be as transitory and illusive to Christian influence as the miner. To the clergy, his character seemed to long remain much the same. W.S. Bell, a Congregational mission executive characterized the cowboy in 1892: "Free-hearted and generous, but wild as the range over which he roams, living in the present, leaving the future to take care of itself, the cowboy is perhaps the most difficult to reach. He gives as the symbol of his life the unbranded steer, or 'maverick' whom nobody owns." He went on to state that "sometime ago a Christian lady asked one if he was a Christian. 'No,' was his reply, 'I am a maverick, the Lord Jesus Christ hasn't got his brand on me yet.'" Edward C. Abbott, himself a cowboy, wrote in his *Recollections* that he was not a Christian, and went on to say of the cowboys: "Ninety per cent of them was infidels. The life they led had a lot to do with that. After you come in contact with nature you get all that stuff knocked out of you—praying to God for aid, divine Providence and so on—because it don't work. You could pray all you damn pleased, but it wouldn't get you water where there wasn't water. Talk about trusting in Providence, hell, if I'd trusted in Providence I'd have starved to death." Through the exhausting toil of the long drive, the cowboy became fiercely independent, and in legend at least was as untainted by civilization as he was unencumbered by Christianity.

With enormous financial success so quickly achieved, Eastern and British capitalists became interested, and soon large livestock corporations came to dominate the scene. This accelerated the multiplication of cattle and sheep in some areas so that the ranges were not only full, but overstocked; and in the rush of livestock interests to realize a profit as large and as quickly as possible no precautions were taken to handle the livestock on the Northern Plains in an unusually dry summer and hard winter. The collapse of the practice of the open range came in the summer and winter of 1886-1887 hard on the heals of a drastic drop in cattle prices and the appearance of confining fences. This tragedy was finalized when a serious drought was followed by ice and snow in such quantities that an impenetrable shield was formed over the open plains. Then that winter the "chinooks," i.e., warm winds, were not strong enough to melt the ice and snow, so that even what grass there was could not be reached. When the directors of one large livestock corporation inquired as to the condition of their starving herd, the occasion prompted a young cowboy by the name of Charles

M. Russell to sketch a postcard illustration entitled: "The Last of 5,000" depicting the one survivor, a gaunt animal, standing in the deep snow watching the coyotes closing in for the kill.

This was the death blow to the open range; and now opened the era of the ranch with its diversified operations, including fenced pastures, hay fields and consequently more permanent settlement. The cowboy had to settle down to care for the cattle in a much more restricted area, and much to his disgust now had to put up hay to assist in feeding the cattle through the long northern winters. The roving cowboy was becoming domesticated, and for some at least this made the possibility of their being branded with the Christian symbol the more likely. George Logan, a Methodist minister with years of experience among the new ranchers and their hired hands gave this advice to young ministers about to come to the Northern Plains to work among the cattlemen:

As a class they are a big-hearted, intelligent set of men. The free life on the open range has a tendency to make them somewhat reckless at times, but many of these have become ranch-owners and are living straight lives. Many are college men, reading Hebrew, Greek and Latin like professors, quoting from prose and poetic authors of whom perhaps you have never heard, and you will have them at your church services; when the collection is taken, they will be very much in evidence, to your material benefit, especially if you have been able to "roundup," "corral," "earmark" and "brand" something to their liking. They are stalwart, open, frank, and despise sham or cant in anyone.

This may somewhat overstate the case, but as the cowboy partially dismounted and consequently took on a more settled way of life, he did become more accessible to the minister of the Gospel. Now the question arose as to whether or not the clergyman could communicate with him and work with him in the building of a distinctive and enduring Western society.

The American ideal of the independent farmer serving as the backbone of the national society was theoretically, at least, given a strong stimulus with the passage of the Homestead Act in 1862. This piece of legislation provided that any adult citizen could claim a quarter section of 160 acres of the surveyed public domain, and after a period of five years' continuous residency could get the final title by filing a few papers and paying from $26 to $34 in fees. This was an improvement over the existant statute which priced 160 acres at $1.25 per acre. This proved to be an unrealistic pattern as far as the Great Plains were concerned, even when variations were made such as the Timber Culture and Desert Land Acts of the 1870s; but it did lure many farmers and would-be-farmers to the post-Civil War New West. For the purposes of denominational expansion this result was seen as a great portent of the future—the building of an eastern Christian civilization in the vast new frontier.

In response to this challenge homesteaders poured into the Great Plains, and traditional denominational extension patterns were utilized. In 1865 a Methodist layman took up a homestead in Clay county, Kansas, and promptly organized a Sunday school. He noted: "there were no school houses in the country. Religious services were held in the cabins and dugouts of the settlers, or in the groves in warm weather. Indian raids were not uncommon."[1] Methodist classes were organized and an occasional homesteader served as local preacher. Then a circuit was formed; this soon was divided into two, each with six or eight appointments. Quarterly meetings were held with the presence of a visiting presiding elder and the pattern emerged of an indigenous church, without help from any society or board until the church extension society began to give help in the erection of buildings, a matter not so easy to take care of locally as it had been in the timbered states farther East, where it had always been a simple matter for the members of any community to chop down trees and build a log house.

The availability of homesteads was augmented by the large grants made to railroads as part of the inducement to extend the iron rails across the nation. These lands were then also made available at relatively low cost to settlers and were advertised in well organized and effective railroad propaganda campaigns. Though there were many abuses of the intended dispersal of public lands, thousands of claims were filed and railroad parcels bought.

In the 1870s the barbed wire fence kept the cattle out of the fields as the Oliver plow successfully turned the Great Plains sod; but neither of these alleviated the basic problem that the arid conditions prevailing in much of the Great Plains did not make feasible the farming practices of the humid Midwest. Nor was it realized what Western winds would do to the soil once it had been exposed by the plow. Also for the settler there was the intense heat of the summer and for those in the Northern reaches, the devastating cold of the winter. A prolonged period of drought after 1879 only exacerbated the situation. This tragedy of miscalculation brought misery and defeat to thousands, and led one mission executive, J.G. Powell, to observe that the area west of the 98th meridian could not be developed as easily as the Plains to the east had been. For there a farmer single-handedly with an ax and plough could clear and break the soil, but what was needed in the Western Plains were skilled engineers and great organizers of capital to lead out its waters into great reservoirs, and then by ditches spread them out upon the fertile soil. The answer of the federal government to this challenge was the opening of section after section of Indian lands, and the Enlarged Homestead Act of 1909, which increased the acreage from 160 to 320 as the basis for a claim. Then in 1912 further accommodation was made in that the time required to prove upon a claim was reduced from five to three years, and of those three years, five months in each could be spent off the claim.

These provisions formed the stimulant to a massive migration into the Great Plains, and when combined with assurances that the newly developed dry land farming methods would be successful, a veritable flood of homesteaders descended upon the area. A decade of wet years seemed to bear out the truth of the glowing predictions, but the weather cycle changed after 1915 and the homesteaders were driven out by continuing drought. But even when the drought abated, there came the man-made disaster of financial bungling. Not only had there been exploitation of natural resources, but the homesteader had exhausted most of the available credit in attempting first to expand his holdings by mortgaging what he already had, and then by borrowing to buy seed and equipment to try anew each year of the drought. The drive to get rich quick, the assumption that farming was easy in the New West, and the misconception that the soils of the Midwest were rapidly becoming exhausted so that the Great Plains was going to be the bread basket of the nation only accelerated the decline of the misdirected homesteader. Like with the open range, the exploitive outlook of making it rich on this frontier advertised as the last chance to make a stake, led to the development of the larger ranch with the necessary capital to construct proper irrigation systems or to buy the equipment to pursue large scale dry land farming.

Many of those who succumbed to the allurements of the advertising depicting the sure successes of life on the Great Plains were ill-equipped to be farmers in the first place. Being city-bred clerks, school teachers, bookkeepers, mechanics and laborers they did not have a single qualification for this kind of life and, of course, failed. Others were farmers from the Midwest who had sustained crop failures or who found the price of land too high to enable them to secure a sufficient acreage to sustain their growing families. Others were immigrants from northern European countries, some of whom were farmers while others were not, but who sought economic advantage in America and came to join their countrymen in this developing area which had room for them. Since so many, especially the American-born, were primarily interested in rapid wealth rather than permanent homes it was their determination to stay only a short time and then return East. Oftentimes these so-called farmers were single men or family men who did not bring their families with them. None of these characteristics were very conducive to the development of Christian congregations as clergy working among the urban immigrants in the Eastern cities were also learning; and when unfavorable conditions prevailed for even a short period of time, it was relatively easy for many to pull up stakes and leave the area thus continuing the high mobility that was such a bane to Christian endeavor.

Among the young families that settled on the lands now being put under the plow came the establishment of homes, and whether permanent or not, here were the fields white unto the harvest for the clergymen. Poignantly expressing this is Ole E. Rolvaag in his novel *Giants in the Earth*. He depicts how the travelling Norwegian Lutheran missionary comes across the small community of sod houses on the Dakota prairie and announced that he is going to hold worship in the largest of these homes. He describes the event among these Norwegian immigrants:

> The minister stood in the corner next to the window, arrayed in full canonicals. The gown was threadbare and badly wrinkled, as a result of its many journeys inside the old valise; the ruff might have been whiter, perhaps; but such trifles were not noticed now, for here stood a real Norwegian minister in ruff and robe! ... The table, spread with a white cloth, had been placed so close to the window that the minister barely had space to stand behind it; on the table stood two homemade candles, one at either end; the candlesticks, too, were homemade, cut from two four-inch pieces of sapling, with the bark left on and painted white; at a little distance they looked like curious works of art.... The pastor read the opening prayer. Then he announced the hymn which they were to sing, and himself led the singing; a few joined in at first,

one voice after another straggling along, like waves on a calm sea; but before the first stanza was ended every voice had picked up the tune and the room was vibrating to a surge of mighty song. After the hymn the minister chanted, conducting the full service just as if it had been a real church.... How wonderful it seemed!... The people sat and stood about while he was preaching, hanging on every word he said. Only a few were competent to climb the ladder of reasoning that he had raised for him. The others realized that he was preaching well, and let it go at that; it gave them a simple satisfaction just to listen; they rejoiced in their hearts that such a man had come here today; they felt that he wished them well.

This longing for the security of the past now idealized in the minds of some living on the wind swept prairies was not to be found among the foreign born only, but also among the emigrant American born. Comments like the following are not uncommon in the diaries and reminiscences of the pioneer homesteaders: "As we sang the old hymns and heard the gospel, there were many eyes dimmed with tears as recollections of the old home and the old home church came to memory." A similar account reads: "Ministers of any denomination were welcomed for preaching services...and almost everybody attended, partly because there were 'so few things to do,' partly because of a hunger for the familiar music and ceremonies and consolation that so many had known in their old homes further east."

Missionary pastors were quick to realize that the lands were being peopled by those who ventured all on the success of the homestead and that these were often an industrious and cultured people, men and women who had been reared in the churches back East and who now give character and tone to frontier communities. It was also observed that on the frontier the churches must reach these people immediately or they will lose their faith. The fact of barbarism seemed to be documented here as well since religious concerns were seemingly so easily trampled underfoot. It came to be the conclusion of those who directed the mission program: "We have no tradition to sustain us." Emphasis was placed upon the New West being essentially a new land where a churchman could not count on the habit of church attendance or rely on loyalty to a denomination. Rather the challenge was to not lay hold on a description of religious experience or ecclesiastical propriety, but religious experience itself freshly felt in the lives of the people and to build up a Christian order from the very foundation stones. Even more pointed was the observation of Josiah Strong, who had pastored the Congregational Church in Cheyenne, Wyoming, in the early 1870s: "The demoralizing atmosphere of the New West is seen in the fact that there are everywhere church members who seem to have left their religion behind when they crossed the Missouri. Many men who lived reputable Christian lives in the East are swept into the great maelstrom of worldliness."

As has been noted, often the key to the success of religious penetration in a specific area was the personality of the local minister. In leaving an Eastern environment of many established traditions, including the institution of the church and the position of the clergy, he entered into and became a part of an emerging society in which he frequently had to erect a place both for himself and for the church. What this meant for the clergyman was that he had to stand on his own merits, and could not even rely on the qualifications of his ordination certificate. Denominational leaders on the frontier repeatedly pointed out this situation, and clergymen who remained for a period of years perceived that this was the case, concurring with the judgment: "A man's denomination and cloth count for very little, but the man counts for the degree of his success or failure."[2] Drawing somewhat of a contrast with the Eastern institutionalized Christianity this mature observation of the New West asserted that: "if a man can show himself devoted to his calling, free from priestly pretention, possessing tact in social relations, with extraordinary common sense and prudence, free from ecclesiastical mannerisms, with a big heart, with love and sympathy for his fellowmen, he will not want for temporal support, and the Lord can be trusted to supply his spiritual bread." This did not deny the need for formal education, as it was often requested by Western congregations, but did accent the need for a perceptiveness of Western life and a flexibility to adapt to local situations without compromising the essentials of the Christian faith. Among the more successful in the New West were those who were impatient with the conventional church of the East and longed for the opportunity to react creatively to new situations; and in this regard youth could be an asset, and also if one were not married his chances of surviving the financial vicissitudes were better; but also important was for the clergyman to exclaim: "Thank God I'm here and by His Grace I'll stay here."

Bishop Daniel S. Tuttle stated of his work: "I visited all the people in their business places or their homes, convinced that pastoral visiting is a stronger force to win souls for Christ then is even the most eloquent preaching." Denominational executives were constantly chiding their men to be actively engaged in cabin and, if need be, saloon visitation. One of the most beloved Western pastors was the Methodist William Wesley Van Orsdel, who conducted a nearly half century ministry in frontier areas of the Northern Plains before his death in 1919. A testimony to the esteem in which he was held by thousands is given in this eulogy:

> Everyone in the entire country knew him, and they knew if he came to a home and the baby was crying and the mother was trying to do the chores, he would pitch into cleaning the barn, milking the cow, cutting wood, or rocking the baby. Or he would churn butter or any other job that needed to be done and he had a way of knowing just what to do to be most helpful. After all these things were taken care of he would get out the well worn Bible and give these hungry folks the word of life. The way he lived before them made him a shining example to all

and especially to those whose lives he had touched in a personal way.[3]

The beginnings of work in any particular area were at times the instigation of faithful lay persons, but most often it was at the behest of a travelling missionary that whatever flicker of Christian communal life present was nurtured. The Methodist Church so successful in the Midwest and South continued its program of the circuit system with itinerant preachers. Compared with the circuits in the old conferences, these frontier circuits were more like the Eastern districts with a missionary presiding over an area of fifty or one hundred miles or more as the only representative of the denomination in that area. This policy of constant ministerial travel secured for the Methodists the honor of being the first to enter, locate and frequently to build in many of the towns of the New West. This policy continued until eventually the circuit rider got around no longer on a saddle horse, light buggy, or train, but rather in a Ford. At the close of World War I it was noted that "the present day circuit rider firmly grips the steering wheel of a Ford, turns on the gas, makes his four appointments a day, ministering to hundreds of hungry hearted people in remote settlements and brings fresh courage and cheer to the regions beyond."[4] There were those Methodists who objected to this system, stating that in the New West whatever interest created at one service seemed to pass away before another occurred, and despite the success of the method in the geographically more compact Midwest, another program was needed in the vast stretches of the Great Plains. This approach was criticized for continuing the eastern concept of the institutional church which served people corporately; while frequently in the New West there was not this community stability nor even an institutional church attitude to undergird this approach. These same complaints had been raised in the Ohio and Mississippi River Valleys in the first half of the nineteenth century; but the denomination clung tenaciously to this pattern as the most efficient and productive it could devise.

The Lutherans also frequently followed the Methodist pattern by establishing extensive circuits of either preaching points or congregations that came under the tutelage of a single pastor, frequently assisted in the summer months by seminary students who preached, called on members, and taught Bible schools, sometimes in English and sometimes in the language of that particular Lutheran ethnic group. Among the Germans particularly, but also to a considerable degree among the Scandinavian Lutherans, the retention of the mother tongue was seen as integral to the continuance of the inherited faith. It did not matter if English was used in business transactions, or in conversation with American neighbors, but in the observance of religion, the language in which the Bible and Luther's catechism had been memorized could not be translated without seemingly doing violence to the content of the faith. Among the Germans especially the development of parochial schools was begun to preserve this heritage. Because of the language situation it was necessary for the Lutheran methodology to be such as to permit a reaching out to every home of a potential Lutheran family. Thus a rather liberal extension policy developed on the far-flung frontier in the attempt to incorporate all of that language background into a common religious community. Just because there was a common language background did in no way assure the positive response to the missionary's efforts. This fact was often lamented by the untiring missionary who was physically expending himself to reach these far-flung countrymen. It was the object of the denomination to gradually divide these widely extended circuits into individual parishes with decreasing numbers of congregations to a parish, with each parish being served by its own pastor.

The Episcopal church developed a new pattern of extension west of the Mississippi River which involved the denomination sending missionary bishops who were to bring the full presence of the church to a frontier area. Furthermore, with national funding, the bishops were not only to carry on their own pastoral ministry, but as administrators to secure and locate priests in selected communities, usually those that were thought to become the urban centers of the future. Thus a conservative approach to missions was carried out, but unlike in much of the Midwest, this denomination was on the scene early and with a bishop, rather than waiting for the development of a diocese in a frontier area to be capped with the election of a bishop supported entirely by the new diocese. The lament was expressed that this policy of concentrating the work in a few sites deprived the denomination of developing roots in the remote rural areas, which became the stronghold of the Methodist Church.

The Congregational and Presbyterian churches continued on a limited scale the practice of comity that had been first enunciated in the early years of the nineteenth century so that these two groups, with such a similar historical background, sought not to duplicate each other's efforts in one place. Yet both groups continued to ply a rather conservative course in the New West, partially because they did not have great numbers of adherents moving into the area, and partially because of the limited funds available to the national mission organizations that were responsible for directing and supporting the work. Also there was frequent tension between the national offices and the men and women on the field as the denominations were slow to take cognizance of the facts of the Western scene. Yet the Congregationalists did think that there would be a rather good response to their understanding of Christianity. Having removed the shackles of creedal orthodoxy, the denominational spokesmen asserted that "our spirit of freedom, democracy and fellowship appeals to Western people and the door is wide open for the organization of as many churches as we can possibly care for." This led to spurts of rapid expansion at the time of the various homesteader onrushes, and in many areas this field soon drastically dried up leaving the denomination with many stifled beginnings. Also the lack of emphasis on denominationalism seemed to work against the preservation of a denominational presence. These denominations, as was traditional with them, sought not only the development of congregations, but expended much effort in the establishment of Sunday schools, often as predecessors to congregational organization, and often seeing these fledging efforts dissolve before more permanent work could be established. Not to be forgotten was higher education as was evidenced in the establishment of colleges which was also typical of their work and that of other denominations back East at an earlier date.

Denominations with a heavy constituency in the former Confederacy found it difficult to support mission endeavors in the New West because of the strapped economic condition of the South. This was particularly lamented by the Baptists and to an extent by the Christians (Disciples of Christ) as many pioneers to the New West came from the former Border States and the South and had roots in these denominations. Unlike much of the work in the Ohio and Mississippi River Valleys, the Baptist expansion was not the result of the efforts of farmer-preachers, but rather of fulltime clergymen funded to a large extent by national missionary agencies. This led to a much more conservative expansion than this large denomination had known prior to the Civil War. Also the denomination had split in the 1840s into Northern and Southern organizations. The Southern Baptists did not undertake work in the New West at this time, and the much smaller Northern Baptist denomination did not undertake work until a relatively late date. The common policy of seizing centers of influence and working out from these put this group into the mold of the conservative expansion pattern. A distinctive technique for outreach was the introduction of the colporteur wagon for use in wide areas of the Great Plains. The colporteur lived in this wagon and visited many small communities which had no pastoral help. This was one way of making contact with widely distributed members and potential members and also dispensing literature. This was later augmented

by fitting out a railroad car as a chapel car for religious services in areas where the railroad penetrated but a Baptist
church had not yet been organized or built. The Christian
(Disciples of Christ) denomination had by this time given up
its opposition to national organization and national programs, but like the Northern Baptists, in beginning quite late
with modest programs it was not able to aggressively prose-
cute large scale work in the New West.

As has already been noted, denominational mission boards
and societies were largely responsible for the undertaking of
mission work in the New West, and the continuance and extension of that work depended very heavily upon the continued financial backing of these organizations. There were
two forms of financial aid: that which aided or provided the
minister's salaries; and that which loaned or donated money
for the erection of church buildings. Conditions for receiving
aid, with exceptions frequently being made, included that
local congregations contribute to their utmost ability, and that
each congregation reduce its request each year or give a reason
for not doing so as had been the policy of the American Home
Mission Society since its founding in 1826. Also it was
incumbant on each Western congregation to seriously attempt
to make contributions to the national programs of the denomination so that while receiving from the parent denomination on a considerable scale, at least on a modest scale with
yearly increases, if possible, it was at the same time contributing to the work of the entire denomination. It was often the
case that national offices could not understand why it was so
expensive to live in the New West and therefore, why Western
congregations were not able to assume more of their own expenses, or why in comparison to other small town and rural
scenes they needed so much money to carry on modest programs. This was part of the nearly constant misunderstanding
and tension that existed between the East and the West.

At times a pro-rata schedule was worked out so that for a
certain amount contributed on the part of the mission congre-

gation there would be a specified support program up to a designated maximum number of dollars. Other times a set number of dollars was provided. Then there were disputes as to who should apportion the funds to specific programs. Some denominations considered this the prerogative of the national office, while Westerners felt just as strongly that the lump sum should be made available to representatives of the denomination in the state or territory as men on the scene could best allot the always meager funds to the best advantage in that area. Occasionally more than one agency in a denomination was funding work in a given area, and it happened at times that they worked at cross purposes with one another bringing forth more denominational bickering.

As to the raising of the local share of the funds, there were widely varying opinions. Rarely were the voluntary contributions of the members sufficient. Occasionally a patron could be found to underwrite the enterprise, but this was most unusual. More than likely an appeal had to be made to the general public based on the assumption that a church was good for the moral life of the community. And if the appeal were being made for the first church in a community, this argument very often met with financial support on the part of many elements of the population. Another frequent approach was through church bazaars and dinners. Especially in communities composed of a large percentage of unmarried men this appeal received generous support. Within the churches themselves, much opposition occurred when the attempt to raise money was based on sponsoring a dance or conducting a raffle. Though this method was sometimes used, it could well be attended by a public behavior that was not at all in tune with the spirit the sponsoring church was seeking to instill into the community.

Attempts to raise money to assist in paying the clergyman's salary were many in number, but the end result, even with mission aid, was such that the total salary was very low in comparison to the cost of living, not infrequently necessitating the clergyman to pursue work beyond his ministerial duties to support his family. Most denominations objected to this, but if it were the only way to keep a man in the ministry carefully stipulated guidelines for extra employment were established.

It was easier to secure community support for the erection of a church building, but since this was a large expenditure in the largely timberless Plains the denominations created separate national boards to gather and distribute church erection funds. It was universally seen as necessary for a congregation to have its own house of worship. Though temporary arrangements to utilize a civic building such as a courthouse or schoolhouse or sometimes even a dance hall might be necessary, the desire for a church was uppermost in the mind of the clergyman and his supporters. Several congregations might for a time share the building that had been erected by one denomination, usually the first one on the scene. However, when it did come time to build, the congregation needed to be as wise as Solomon in selecting the proper site, though this was often compromised if a railroad company or a town site company offered a free lot with the stipulation that a building of stated value be built within a specified time. Once it had been determined that it was feasible to build, and this might indeed be a misjudgment, a fact witnessed to by the buildings giving mute testimony to a Christian presence in ghost towns, the type of building was a prime consideration. To make an impression on the community it could not be too unpretentious a structure, yet the funding often would not allow a more elaborate construction. Congregations suffered from both poor buildings that were long if ever in being replaced, and from expensive houses of worship that saddled the congregations and church erection societies with cumbersome debts for years, perhaps even beyond the lives of the individual congregations. Perceptive was the minister and congregation that could accurately judge the present needs and build accordingly, and still have the flexibility to meet the needs of a succeeding generation. If it had not been for the continual, if somewhat fluctuating, presence of national funds, most of these building enterprises would have been significantly delayed or never even begun.

In spite of these financial difficulties the national pattern of denominational competition continued. In a nation where religious freedom meant that there was no restriction on religious belief and its propagation through local organizations, which also enjoyed freedom from civic responsibility in regard to their finances and properties coming under any form of taxation, the door was open for the establishment even on the sparsely settled frontier of a large number of Christian groups which had far more in common than that which differentiated them from one another. Sometimes the rather minute differences had to be enlarged to justify before the unchurched majority what the reason was for this seemingly ridiculous competition.

On the frontier this intense competition for souls was not likely to take place immediately, but if the population rose and the semblance of more permanent settlement patterns emerged the possibility of over-churching an area increased. Some denominations sought not to duplicate their work as was the case already noted between the Congregationalists and Presbyterians. Some other denominations of an Anglo-Saxon background were sensitive to not entering a field if other Anglo-Saxon groups were already there, but this was more the exception than the rule. The immigrant ethnic churches were unaware of this as they went in search of their own, regardless of how many other missions were already operating. Finally by the time of World War I serious consideration was being given both regionally and nationally to a program of comity, i.e., designated areas would be surveyed and with these results a certain denomination would be assigned a specific area and other churches, usually the latter ones to arrive, would be asked to abandon the field, or trade congregations by being given priority in another area. Also in areas where no one had started work, a denomination would be asked to undertake pioneer religious endeavors. While this looks reasonable on paper, it was at times hard to implement, though it did recognize that the frontier era was closing, and that the mistakes of congregational multiplication in a given community that were so prominent back East should be avoided if at all possible. With the determined effort to work out comity arrangements, denominations in the New West had struggled through the vicissitudes of pioneer settlement and were seeking to present to the still largely untouched population a sense of maturity in the developing of a Western American culture.

The attitudes and methodologies of the older frontiers often did not work well in Great Plains and Intermountain West, but by the time this was recognized the frontier had basically disappeared; the statement to this effect being that sentence in the census report of 1890: "The unsettled area has been so broken into by isolated bodies of settlement that there can hardly be said to be a frontier line." There was also considerable tardiness in reaction to the plight of the farmers, even more so than in reaction to the urban scene. The denominations did not come to the support of William Jennings Bryan and his espousal of the Populist cause in the 1890's as they did to the urban programs of Theodore Roosevelt and later Woodrow Wilson. Even though the Protestant churches are considered rural in their orientation, it is not until well after World War I that the denominations seek to address themselves to agrarian discontent. The Protestant churches prior to World War I were simply silent on the plight and problems of the farmer, but were struggling to establish themselves in the vast agricultural areas.

It was not only the work among the new white inhabitants of the Great Plains and Intermountain West that proved to be so difficult; an even more difficult task, when undertaken at all, was the attempt to spread the Christian faith among the roving Indians, who in 1871 with the abolition of the treaty system came to be considered as wards of the government rather than free men. In 1872 Brother Van, as William Wesley Van Orsdel was affectionately called, disembarked the steamer *Far West* at Fort Benton, Montana, in answer to his Macedonian Vision to preach to the bronzed inhabitants which he envisioned standing with their arms stretched heavenward pleading for the blessings of God. When Van had been in the New West only a short time, he learned that his vision had not been well founded, in spite of the widely disseminated account of the four Flathead Indians who had crossed the Great Plains from the Rocky Mountains in search of the "white man's book", which led to the initiation of a serious Protestant endeavor in Oregon in the 1830s to compliment the Roman Catholic missions already underway. What Van discovered was a red man that was not interested in Christianity, in part because of the behavior of the supposedly Christian white men; and Van himself soon realized that he could not accomplish much with the red man if the white man continued to live as he did. He never forgot his mission to the Indians, and tried to spend some time with them every year, such as celebrating the Fourth of July with the tribe at Browning, Montana; but the bulk of his extensive endeavors was spent among the white men. Just before the fourth anniversary of his arrival occurred the Battle of the Little Big Horn, where an ambitious army officer led his forces into annihilation at the hands of the warriers of Sitting Bull who refused to remain on reservations established for them; and then a year after Custer's defeat, Brother Van served as a civilian scout to aid the terrified settlers in the path of the illusive Chief Joseph as he led his Nez Percé on a circuitous route in search of freedom that failed of accomplishment almost within sight of the Canadian border. Whether the Indian was lashing back or was simply seeking to escape to another land, the white settlers were in no mood to have him included in their new land; and the Indian, for his part, had no desire to be Christianized, as this was usually presented as part of a civilizing force that also required him to settle down and adopt the white man's way of life, where he was not even welcome. The result of this was that after the Indian's short lived triumph at the Little Big Horn, the American people rallied to put an end to the Indian menace; and by 1885 all but a few Indians were living on reservations, and by 1910 his numbers had been reduced from the total of one million that had roamed the land when Columbus first arrived to 265,000 living in widely scattered and frequently small units, with about half to be found in Oklahoma, Arizona, New Mexico and South Dakota. With the surrender of Geronimo in 1886, the end of serious fighting by the Plains Indians had come, but the white man's slaughter did not end until the panicked troops sent in to disarm the Sioux attending a religious ceremonial at Wounded Knee, South Dakota, in 1890, killed nearly one hundred and fifty, many of them women and children.

Some work among the native Americans in the New West was done; and an impetus for this was the Indian policy initiated by President Grant in 1869. This "peace policy" provided for a reform of the Indian Bureau that included charging the churches with nominating and supervising Indian agents. This inaugurated a close cooperation between the churches and the state that led the Commissioner of Indian Affairs to state as late as 1928: "It is quite safe to venture the assertion that the Church and State are more closely associated in the Indian country than is the case elsewhere." The Quakers in particular, long noted for their work among the Indians, were the most active in this arrangement, but the Christian churches as a whole did not aggressively respond to the challenge. In 1881 Helen Hunt Jackson sought to prick the conscience of America in her indictment of the treatment of the Indian published under the title : *A Century of Dishonor*. Six years later remedial action was presumed taken with the passage of the Dawes Act, wherein the reservations were

divided into 160-acre family farms so that the Indians could
be readily indoctrinated into white middle class American
virtues. This overt attempt to conform the Indian to the
American way of life in fact obliterated the Indian tribal
society which gave meaning to the lives of the red men. The
response of the churches to this step was generally favorable.
The Christian community saw this method of acculturation
as preparing the environment wherein the churches could
carry on mission work on the same basis that they were using
with the white settlers. There was little attempt to understand
the native Indian culture, or to integrate the Christian faith
within this culture. The program ultimately failed to force
the red man to become a white man on purely economic
terms, as the attempt to allocate small parcels of reservation
land, which was marginal in the first place, proved disastrous. The farming programs of the humid forested and
grassy plains of the Midwest worked no better for the Indian
than it was to succeed among the white homesteaders on the
arid Plains. Also, as with the Homestead Act for white settlement, there was built into the program the possibility of
misuse so that large amounts of land did not end up in the
hands of those for whom it had been intended.

With the country feeling it had solved the pesky Indian
problem, the plight of the Indian soon fell from the sight of
the church members as well. While no denomination was to
undertake large scale work among them, the most noted
efforts were those of the Southern Methodists in Oklahoma
and the Roman Catholics in the Southwest, with important
missions also being operated by the Northern Methodists,
Baptists, Presbyterians and Episcopalians. As a result of the
work that was done one-third of the remaining Indian population was to be found within the institutionalized Christian
churches by the time of World War I; this despite a movement in the 1890s, known as the "Ghost Dance," wherein
Messianic, pacifistic and apocalyptic cults combined Christian and native elements to teach about a time when the aged,

weary earth would die and be reborn, with the white man to another world and the red man to their undisturbed lands of old. Again policies of an earlier time and in a different place proved somewhat inadequate; and especially so when the denominations themselves, like the American people in general, did not have a sympathetic interest in the intended benefactors of this mission. Yet the numbers of Indians that were counted within the Christian faith gives testimony that work was accomplished which cannot be discounted.

6

The Crusading Spirit

In 1835, Lyman Beecher, the father of Henry Ward Beecher, asserted in a missionary tract entitled *Plea for the West* that the future of the nation and the world was to be determined by the emerging character of the Ohio-Mississippi River Valley when he stated: "the West is destined to be the great central power of the nation, and under heaven, must affect powerfully the cause of free institutions and the liberty of the world." He therefore implored the Protestant denominations to as quickly as possible missionize this area in order that the nation could be preserved in an Anglo-Saxon Protestant mold. Just fifty years later, Josiah Strong, in a similar missionary tract entitled, *Our Country*, put the plea on a broader basis: the future of mankind depends upon the Anglo-Saxons. This is so because the Anglo-Saxons, by which he meant the stock that had resulted from the comingling of the various peoples who had come to America, have developed the two divine concepts of civil liberty and a pure spiritual Christianity; and since in America these have been perfected, it is upon the American Protestant community that the destiny of man depends. Almost a decade and a half before the Spanish-American War, Strong noted that the tool of God's civilizing and religious force had been prepared; and at the same time the world was being readied for this crusade. Poems such as Walt Whitman's "Passage to India" and Rudyard Kipling's "White Man's Burden" helped popularize the "manifest destiny" of America that was also being increasingly heralded by politicians and businessmen, albeit, each with their own objectives in mind.

The Spanish-American War, lasting but a few months in 1898, was the spark that ignited the ready torch of American imperialism. The situation in Cuba was also a natural one for the protagonists of America's destiny under God. Here was the task of freeing the Cubans from the misrule of the monarchial, Latin and Roman Catholic Spaniards. It was the urging of such sensationalist papers as the Hearst and Pulitzer publications, who luridly brought to the attention of the American public stories of Cuban mistreatment whether they were factual or not, that readied the imperialist sentiment for ignition. Then on February 15, 1898, a tremendous explosion destroyed the *U.S.S. Maine* as it lay in the port of Havana while making a "courtesy" call. The blast was trumpeted in American newspapers and the reaction was swift, though the actual cause of the explosion, which took the lives of 260 of the 350 men aboard, still remains a mystery. Events now moved quickly, and on April 19 Congress declared Cuba independent and authorized a reluctant President McKinley to use the army and navy to guarantee that independence. Following the expected break of diplomatic relations with Spain, Congress on April 25 declared that a state of war existed.

Less than a week later, Commodore George Dewey, commanding a small squadron, slipped into Manila Bay in the far off Phillipines, surprised the Spanish Pacific fleet and won a startling victory. This event was also sensationally depicted, and called to the attention of the American people a largely unknown chain of distant islands, thus raising the question as to what is the nation's responsibility in that far corner of the world. In nearby Cuba the story was also stunning: American military confusion was saved by the defeat of the Spanish Atlantic fleet and the courageous fighting of a few men such as the over-publicized "Rough Riders" under the command of Theodore Roosevelt. With the threat of tropical disease looming more deadly every day, it was fortunate that Santiago fell on July 17 and that on August 12 the Spanish signed a preliminary peace.

In spite of the enthusiasm that had been engendered for the war, the nation's leaders were soon polarized over what to do with the areas of the Spanish empire now in American hands. One of the most troubled was President McKinley. In October he instructed the American peace commissioners to demand the Philippines. Later he explained his decision to a visiting clerical delegation: "I walked the floor of the White House night after night until midnight; and I am not ashamed to tell you, gentlemen, that I went down on my knees and prayed Almighty God for light and guidance more than one night. And one night it came to me this way—I don't know how it was, but it came . . . there was nothing left for us to do but to take them all, and to educate the Filipinos, and uplift and civilize and Christianize them, and by God's grace to do the best we could by them . . . And then I went to bed, and went to sleep, and slept soundly."

In February the Senate approved the treaty including the acquisition of the Philippines; but the approval was by only one vote above the necessary two-thirds. One of the most vocal supporters of this decision was Senator Albert J. Beveridge, who stated:

> It is destiny that the world shall be rescued from its natural wilderness and from savage men. Civilization is no less an evolution than the changing forms of animal and vegetable life. Surely and steadily the reign of law, which is the very spirit of liberty, takes the place of arbitrary caprice. Surely and steadily the methods of social order are bringing the whole earth under their subjection. And to deny that this is right, is to deny that civilization should increase. In this great work the American people must have their part. They are fitted for the work

as no people have ever been fitted; and their work lies before them.

With regard to the Philippines, he states succinctly: "When circumstance has raised our flag above them, we dare not turn these misguided children over to destruction by themselves or spoliation by others, and then make answer when the God of nations requires them at our hands, 'Am I my brother's keeper?'" Using another Biblical analogy, he becomes even more religiously pointed: "We will not renounce our part in the mission of the race, trustees under God of the civilization of the world....He has marked the American people as his chosen nation to finally lead in the regeneration of the world. This is the divine mission of America....The judgment of the Master is upon us: 'Ye have been faithful over a few things; I will make you ruler over many things.'" In the first instance, the senator was attacking the fundamentalist as well as presidential aspirant, William Jennings Bryan; and in the second he was using the imagery of Andrew Carnegie, who was himself a staunch anti-imperialist.

Articulating the anti-imperialist argument, and also demonstrating how Scripture can be used to fortify this position as well, was Senator George F. Hoar, who responded to Beveridge by quoting: "The Devil taketh him up into an extremely high mountain and showeth him all the kingdoms of the world and the glory of them and saith unto him, 'All these things will be thine if you wilt fall down and worship me.'" In spite of the victory of the war hawks and imperialists at the moment, it was of short duration; for the country returned to a nonimperialistic stance, and as the years passed, it reduced its overseas holdings rather than increasing them. Yet America now realized that she was a world power, and while she did not wish to develop a political empire, she remained very much concerned about influencing the world and attempting to mold it after her own pattern, indicating that she did desire an ideological empire.

While it is not possible to determine with precision how the American churchmen thought with regard to this war, the religious press, usually more forward than the denominational assemblies themselves, can give some clues. This press did not respond with the hysteria of the Hearst and Pulitzer papers to the sinking of the *Maine*, but rather urged restraint so that all the facts could be gathered. Specifically this press did not see the sinking as an excuse for war. While realizing that conditions frequently were deplorable in Cuba, the religious press encouraged the United States government to do what it could for humanitarian reasons. War was not the answer, and the secular press that was clamoring for war was denounced; but once war had come the religious press, joined by convention resolutions and sermons, called for loyalty to the government. By then it was realized that all other avenues of approach to the Cuban problem had been unsuccessfully tried. Typical is this statement in the *Christian-Evangelist* on May 12, 1898: "It is a war in the interest of humanity and of the rights of the oppressed. It is a war that looks to peace... Its disinterestedness appeals to the moral sentiment of mankind, and future historians can but vindicate the justice and righteousness of our cause." When the reports of military victories were widely heralded in the newspapers, the denominational and interdenominational journals began to see the hand of Divine Providence; and while hoping for an early peace, could also now readily justify the war and at the same time issue the call to Protestant mission forces to prepare for work in new fields. The fact that there was a long tradition of Roman Catholicism in these Spanish colonies was only an added incentive to address the missionary opportunities at hand. This call to mission endeavors, however, was clearly a result of the progress of the war, not a reason to instigate it. The religious press was as divided as the nation over the final political solution, but for the moment the expansionists gained the ascendency; and it was this emphasis that gained the ear of

President McKinley, a devout Methodist, who was very sensitive to the voice of the religious press. A press that could ask as did the *Christian-Evangelist* on May 26, 1898: "Are we justified, with all our wealth, our power, our educational and religious development, our civil and religious liberty, our free institutions, in maintaining an isolated position and standing aloof from the great tasks which the civilized nations of the earth must perform in behalf of the world's progress?" The challenge was there.

The Philippines presented a mission field, where, for the first time, foreign work was to be pursued under the American flag, and by 1902 five Protestant denominations worked out a comity pattern for the work that was now to take place in the former Spanish possessions, and thus the denominations accepted the challenge to carry forth the Anglo-Saxon destiny to newly gained territories.

In 1917 Woodrow Wilson, son of a Presbyterian clergyman, occupied the White House and like McKinley before him, was reluctant to lead the nation into war. In fact, Wilson had been elected to his second term on the slogan: "He kept us out of war." Yet, unlike McKinley, who at the outset of the Spanish-American War was an isolationist, Wilson was from the beginning of his administration an active believer in the role of the United States in the world at large. With the ardour of a crusader, Wilson believed that America's primary role was to guide the world's onward march to democracy.

When World War I broke out, American reactions were mixed, and Wilson exhorted his countrymen to retain an attitude of impartiality. He diligently sought to see that nothing should disturb this mood of noninvolvement. Through the months of tension caused by the German submarine activity leading to the loss of American lives, as seen dramatically in the sinking of the luxury liner, *Lusitania*, on May 7, 1915, Wilson continued to seek a way to keep his nation out of the war, and yet preserve a sense of high moral justice. Criticisms grew louder, not only in Congress, but from the press and also from the public. Yet Wilson clung to his high moral purposes and sought to bring the conflict to a close by arbitration. Nonetheless, this effort failed; and even as American opinion began to shift, America's involvement in the conflict rested ultimately in German hands. If they provoked the United States through the sinking of American vessels, Wilson as a man of principle would have to ask Congress for a declaration of war. On January 31, 1917, Germany announced that in its efforts to achieve military victory, it was launching unrestricted submarine warfare. On February 3 Wilson informed Congress that he had severed diplomatic relations with Germany, but was still seeking to avoid American involvement in the war. By this time the fever for war was no longer confined to a vocal and slowly growing minority; yet the sentiment for peace remained powerful. The majority of the people seemingly trusted the president to make the right decision, and were willing to back up that trust by following his leadership. Wilson was thus not persuaded by public opinion, but was in fact able to significantly form this opinion. On April 2, 1917, seeing no other possible response to the sinkings in retaining his moral principles, Wilson asked a joint session of Congress for a declaration of war; and talking with the fervor of a crusader declared that it was America's intention to make the world "safe for democracy." This was to be a war to end all wars. Wilson stated it this way: "We shall fight for the things which we have always carried nearest our hearts—for democracy, for the right of those who submit to authority to have a voice in their own Governments, for the rights and liberties of small nations,' for a universal dominion of right by such a concert of free peoples as shall bring peace and safety to all nations, and make the world itself at last free."

American clergymen became leading spokesmen promoting the righteousness of the nation's war effort. They drew freely on religious traditions of Israelite war, holy crusades, and the "just war" theory. In becoming some of Wilson's best supporters for this noble effort, they spelled out that a holy American force was moving against an altogether evil force. Vividly portraying this was Billy Sunday, whose exhortations for patriotism were joined with such deprecations of the Germans as: "If you turn hell upside down, you will find 'Made in Germany' stamped on the bottom;" or, as he stated in a prayer in the House of Representatives in January, 1918: "Thou knowest, O Lord, that no nation so infamous, vile, greedy, sensuous, blood-thirsty, ever disgraced the pages of history. Make bare thy mighty arm, O Lord, and smite the hungry, wolfish Hun, whose fangs drip with blood, and we will forever raise our voice to thy praise." Primarily, churchmen advocated that the war effort, though it entailed great sacrifices, was the fulfillment of American destiny. Comparing the American crusade with those of earlier centuries, Lyman Abbot stated in a book entitled *The Twentieth Century Crusade*: "A crusade to make this world a home in which God's children can live in peace and safety is more Christian than a crusade to recover from pagans the tomb in which the body of Christ was buried." The individual's responsibility was clearly outlined by Cardinal Gibbons when he told a group of newsmen in April, 1917: "The primary duty of a citizen is loyalty to country. This loyalty is manifested more by acts than by words; by solemn service rather than by empty declaration. It is exhibited by an absolute and unreserved obedience to his country's call." So also denomination vied with denomination to be the more patriotic and to express their intent to aid in their nation's high calling under God in this crusade, as for example the resolution adopted by the Northern Baptist Convention in 1917: "Whereas our country is at war in defense of humanity, liberty and democracy ... we do solemnly pledge to the President and government of the United States our whole-hearted allegiance and support and dedicate ourselves to our just and righteous cause."

Another example of the tendency to merge Protestantism and Americanism during the half century following the Civil War is seen in the foreign mission movement. While most of the denominations had been conducting organized mission work in foreign fields long before the Civil War, it was not until after that event that political and economic developments in those lands made it possible to conduct large scale work. Though the movement had become tempered by the revivalistic emphasis on the necessity of the instantaneous conversion, there also came to the forefront the urgency of the task in extending the domination of Anglo-Saxon Protestantism. Josiah Strong put it this way in 1886: "I believe it is fully in the hands of Christians of the United States during the next ten or fifteen years, to hasten or retard the coming of Christ's kingdom in the world by hundreds and perhaps thousands, of years."

In Latin America there was more political stability and freedom of conscience after 1850, and quickly Protestant mission work was enlarged and made significant gains throughout much of the continent. Work in Moslem areas continued to be very difficult, because, according to strict Moslem codes, Christians might not evangelize in their territories; so while Christian work in the Near East and in North Africa was very slow, Christian missions in Equatorial and South Africa moved ahead after the middle of the century when western powers began to invade the interior of the continent, and here there were no restrictions. In India, the missionary efforts were greatly affected by the political developments; and when in 1857 the English government assumed direct control over the country and gave support to missionary programs, American Protestant missions entered and flourished. Southeast Asia, though hampered by the Buddhist tendency to absorb Christian ideas into the traditional religion, also witnessed flourishing missions at this time. China, like India, was an area where the political situation was very important to the mission programs; and it was not until the Anglo-Chinese wars were ended in 1864 that the interior of the country was opened to mission advance, and several American Protestant denominations entered. After a treaty with the Korean government in 1883 a number of denominations entered this land; and in Japan, after the restoration of government by the Emperor Meiji in 1867, Protestant missions flourished.

The world then appeared to be "white unto the harvest" when a series of developments in America itself propelled the Protestant community to take action, making the last decade of the nineteenth and the first two decades of the twentieth centuries the climactic phase of the foreign missions movement in American Protestantism. The stimulus and leadership for a major portion of this surge of interest rested on the shoulders of D.L. Moody. Climaxing his American college revival in 1886 was the evangelist's invitation to interested students to attend a conference that summer at his school called Mt. Hermon, near his home in Northfield, Massachusetts. Moody had been reluctant to engage in college revivals, thinking that his work was directed toward those who did not have the benefit of a formal education. What he did not realize was that the college-age young people overlooked his grammatical errors and other signs of educational deficiency, and were deeply impressed by his integrity, commitment and enthusiasm. The conference, unintentionally, turned into a discussion of the mission problem, and one of the addresses, entitled "All Should Go and Go to All" made such a profound impression that by the end of the month long meeting, an even one hundred of the two-hundred-fifty students attending took the pledge to become foreign missionaries. By the time of the next summer school, the number had climbed to twenty-one hundred; and in 1888 a permanent organization came into being to implement these commitments. This organization, the Student Volunteer Movement for Foreign Missions, was one of the most important contributions of American Protestantism to world Christianity. The chairman was a young man who was present at Mt. Hermon that first summer, John R. Mott. Under his leadership the Student Volunteer Movement quickly grew and became the most important movement in American student life, drawing together large numbers of young people where they were enlisted for foreign mission work under the theme: "The Evangelization of the World in This Generation." Through the efforts of the Student Volunteer Movement, a high percentage of men destined to become missionary leaders in the twentieth century were recruited. Since Mott was also from 1890 to 1915 the national secretary of the YMCA, he enlarged the involvement already begun by Moody in evangelism programs and now particularly in the establishment of YMCAs in foreign lands to further the mission program.

When success attended the stimulus now given foreign mission work by the political conditions abroad and the Student Volunteer Movement at home, a means of interdenominational coordination seemed essential. This resulted in the creation of the Foreign Missions Conference of North America in 1893, which eventually included the vast majority of Protestant missionary societies in the United States and Canada. Its annual meetings were for the discussion of mutual problems and opportunities, and in a number of cases this led to interdenominational work on specific fields. In 1902 the Missionary Education Movement was begun, and soon forty-seven denominations were affiliated in this enterprise of publishing missionary literature to keep the growing needs of the enterprise before the American public. Another agency to implement the mission thrust was the organization in 1906 of the Layman's Missionary Movement, which not only sought to propagate the mission idea, but to secure financial support for such programs. This was in addition to the enormous support that was being given by women's auxiliaries that had been formed in the churches for this express purpose, and for giving the women a tangible objective to pursue in denominational work. Mark Twain's character of Senator Dilworthy would not let such a woman's meeting go unnoticed when he was back home among the people: "He graced the sewing circles of the ladies with his presence, and even took a needle now and then and made a stitch or two upon a calico shirt for some poor Bible-less pagan of the south Seas, and this act enchanted the ladies, who regarded the garments thus honored as in a manner sanctified." These movements came to a climax prior to World War I, with the formation of the International Missionary Council which was an outgrowth of the 1910 World Missionary Conference in Edinburgh. There was now developing an international agency to implement the mission surge that had developed in both Western Europe and America.

The evangelistic religious motivation coupled with a sense of Anglo-Saxon destiny for foreign missions was abetted after the Spanish-American War with a distinct tinge of American imperialism. The line of demarcation between complete personal commitment and evangelistic imperialism is sometimes very narrow, whether this commitment be to traditional revivalistic Protestantism or the humanitarian concerns that were understood to underlie the American way of life. Democratic and humanitarian sentiment came to the fore as reasons for support of these programs and particularly so for work in the newly won dependencies. Robert Speer, a leader in the Student Volunteer Movement, summed this up in 1910 by stating that the great need for the world was "to be saved from want and disease and injustice and inequality and impurity and lust and hopelessness and fear." So potent was this challenge that between 1899 and 1914, a total of 4,521 missionaries left American shores for foreign work, and the United States took over the leadership in the foreign mission enterprise both in terms of funds and manpower. It is remarkable, however, that the missionary endeavors themselves were involved in so little of imperialism, even though this connection was widely heralded at home as seen in this statement in the *Methodist Review* in September, 1898: "There is no chance to shut one's eyes to the relation of missions to the success of governmental colonizing schemes." Even though nationalism provided a powerful incentive to the development of the missionary movement, it remained secondary to the spiritual and theological motivation. American missionaries simply did not try to create an American empire abroad though their secular counterparts were bent on an American business empire. The missionaries were often perplexed as to how to convey the Christian message in any form other than their familiar American pattern. In this regard, their efforts did at times lead toward Americanization as well as Protestantization; but they were also sensitive to the Gospel's universality, including its capacity of being proclaimed and practiced in a variety of native settings. As long as this realization was kept to the forefront in their thinking, the American missionaries had considerable chance of success; but when they fell back on advantages to be obtained because of their government's or some European government's presence, much of their effectiveness was lost. The recognition of this by missionaries in the fields led to the appreciation of the importance of native leadership, which was expressed in the first decade of the new century by the founding of indigenous churches in Japan and India.

Prior to World War I, the foreign mission story is almost totally a Protestant narrative. American Roman Catholics supported by monetary contributions the world-wide missions of the Church; but as late as 1906 only about a half dozen American Roman Catholics were serving in foreign fields. It was only in 1908 that America was removed from the status of being a mission field itself, and four years later the first American society dedicated to foreign missions, Catholic Foreign Mission Society of America, or Maryknoll, was founded, and it was not until 1918 that the first priests were commissioned for work in China.

As with other aspects of the American religious scene, World War I was a turning point. After the war the mission movement was to become inextricably entangled in other issues, notably the struggle between the fundamentalists and liberals that rose to such a fever pitch in the 1920s. Yet until the outbreak of the war, the crusade for missions was another instance of American Protestantism, shaping and being shaped by its national environment, giving expression to the optimistic creed that God was calling America for a specific task.

With America carrying out its destiny abroad, there remained the serious challenge to make sure that the Anglo-Saxon Protestant faith was securely anchored at home. A vibrant crusade addressed to this continuing task was the promotion of the Sunday school. At its beginnings in Gloucester, England, in 1780 and in the first Sunday school in America five years later, this program had sought to give a rudimentary education to the poor who were unable to secure basic education; but increasingly the schools devoted their energies to imparting basic religious knowledge primarily through the extensive memorization of Biblical passages. The Sunday school also came to be regarded as a prime instrument for the inculcation of middle class American virtures. Again Twain's Senator Dilworthy epitomized this in a visit to a frontier town when "he touched reverently upon the institutions of religion, and upon the necessity of private purity, if we were to have any public morality. 'I trust,' he said, 'that there are children within the sound of my voice,' and after some remarks to them, the Senator closed with an apostrophe to 'the genius of American liberty, walking with the Sunday-school in one hand and Temperance in the other up the glorified steps of the National capitol."

One of the prime movers in the immediate post-Civil War Sunday school movement was once again D.L. Moody. The school that he developed in Chicago became one of the largest in the United States, and he used many devices to gather together the children of the Chicago slums to attend this school. His son recounts: "In his recruiting excursions his pockets were almost always filled with oranges, candy, maple sugar, or something toothsome. At one time he offered a squirrel with its cage to the one who would bring in the largest number of scholars within a specified time." Having enticed them into the school, often himself securing the parents' consent, he worked hard to keep them there. He did this by personally looking after them, visiting in the homes when they missed, and showing such a warm, personal interest in them that many became devotedly attached to him.

Moody was also a prime mover in the development of Sunday school conventions to improve the quality of teaching methods, content, and administration. At these inter-denominational events organized on city, county, state and national levels, teachers were enlisted, trained and inspired to revitalize the Sunday school into an ever more efficient evangelism tool. In 1872, the editor of the Methodist Sunday school publications, John H. Vincent, proposed the adoption of the Uniform Lesson Plan. Replacing the strictly catechetical approach of memorization, this approach called for each class, regardless of age level, in every Sunday school participating in the program to be studying the same lesson on the same Sunday. This plan was widely adopted in a very short time; and the common lesson became a bond of union, not only within the individual school, but between the different schools in a single community as well as across the nation. It was also an aid to teacher preparation as the instructors in the participating schools could gather at a single location to study and prepare next Sunday's lesson, as well as facilitating the production and distribution of the Biblical materials pertinent to the lessons.

More elaborate preparations for teachers than the enthusiasm of the conventions, or the Saturday afternoon community lesson planning sessions were provided in the establishment of teacher-training institutes. This idea also caught on quickly and spread across the country. Vincent was also the spearhead of this idea, and beginning in 1874 he took over an old camp meeting ground on the shores of Lake Chautauqua in New York to bring together a group of Sunday school teachers for a combined two weeks' training course and recreation period. This soon developed into an all-summer program addressing a variety of themes; and then developed an extensive program of correspondence courses; and finally added an elaborate network of traveling Chautauquas bringing culture and entertainment to the nation's towns and villages. "Chautauqua was, more than any other agency, an expression of the great popular desire to coordinate culture with religion and a means of giving to that desire of millions all the literary and scientific culture that they had time or training to receive."[1] Retaining a more distinctly Bible training approach was the effort of D.L. Moody in the establishment of the Moody Bible Institute in Chicago in 1886. Here programs were developed to supplement the education received at colleges or theological seminaries by a thorough study of the English Bible and in methods of aggressive Christian work. Additional preparation for those already engaged in some form of the ministry was available at the Institute; and provision was made to give a larger acquaintance with the Bible and methods of Christian effort for those who desired to devote part of their time to religious work.

Within a brief period of time, the revitalized Sunday school began to replace the traditional revival as the primary recruiting device of the churches, sometimes even becoming a competitive religious agency with classes for adults as well as children. The American entrepreneurial spirit is seen in the development of such crusading slogans as "Each One Win One," as it was the duty of the students to bring in other students; and then the program was developed so that the entire year of the school was pointed toward "Decision Day" which was the counterpart to the revivalist's altar call. So successful was the Sunday school movement in developing techniques that by the opening decade of the twentieth century cities across America competed for the privilege of holding Sunday school conventions, so popular and influential had these schools become in the shaping of the Protestant American character.

Questions, however, were raised about the adequacy of the Uniform Lesson Plan; such questions as to the advisibility of all age levels studying the same topic, the lack of denominational emphasis in the nondenominational lessons, and the almost total neglect of the liturgical year. To answer some of these questions there appeared in 1910 a closely graded series of lessons, with separate study materials for each grade or year. Also the solitary emphasis on the Bible was broken by some use of other materials from the history of the faith. Some denominations began to prepare their own materials, insisting that educational materials be under the careful scrutiny of the individual denomination. Many schools continued to use the Uniform Lesson Plan, and continued to do so when elements of the closely graded series were incorporated in a series known after 1918 as the International Improved Uniform Lessons.

Augmenting the more formal activities of the Sunday school were programs designed especially for the youth. Originating in 1881 was the nondenominational Christian Endeavor Young Peoples' Society, a self-managed society of young people above the age of twelve for worship and instruction. Though this nondenominational society continued, it was increasingly challenged by strictly denominational organizations such as the Methodist Epworth League, formed in 1889; the Baptist Young People's Union, established in 1891; and the Luther League, begun in 1895. Also independent of the Sunday school was the Vacation Bible school, founded in New York in 1901, and within a few years becoming national in scope. Though avowedly Protestant, but often intensely denominational in tone, all of these educational endeavors were thought to be composed of loyal Americans as well as devout Christians nurturing the Anglo-Saxon Protestant character.

While the Sunday school and other youth organizations represent a positive thrust into the American scene, there was also within American Protestantism a strong negative strain; a factor clearly seen in the re-emergence of a spirit of nativism that sought to curb the influence of Roman Catholicism. Concern over the rapidly increasing presence of Roman Catholicism, especially the new immigrants from Southern and Eastern Europe, was expressed on many levels. Social apprehensions were raised by the poverty, illiteracy, and unsanitary habits of many of the new immigrants. Cultural concern was expressed at the differing folkways, customs, mores, and patterns of behavior that these Roman Catholics exhibited. The political impact was greatly feared, as expressed in the comment concerning the immigrant: "landed on Monday and voted on Tuesday;" which meant that these people were met at the dock by the "bosses", quickly registered, and then shepherded to the polls, as part of the alleged manipulative process by which they gained employment. Asserting an ecclesiastical control of votes, Josiah Strong stated: "The Roman Catholic vote is more or less perfectly controlled by the priests. That means that the Pope can dictate some hundreds of thousands of votes in the United States." Another serious concern was the economic fact that many of these people did indeed provide cheap labor for an expanding America, which tended to depress wages for the native born. All of these fears and concerns suggested to old stock Americans that there was a serious alien intrusion into the national life, and that in order to prevent a collapse of the America they had known, this immigration must be checked; and in the meantime the influence of these people sharply reduced. So prevelant was this anti-Catholicism that an editorial in the *Chicago Tribune* on October 10, 1873, stated: "We suppose that not one third of the men or women brought up in evangelical churches in this country ever heard a kind word said in their youth concerning the Catholic faith, though they have all heard this church denounced as the 'Scarlet Woman,' and if the Catholic laity escaped like excoriation, it was on the ground that they were too ignorant and too priest-ridden to know any better."

It was in the political arena that the nativist attack on the problem was highly organized. The "Know-Nothing" party, which had exemplified this point of view before the Civil War, had collapsed during that struggle; but it was not long after the cessation of hostilities that other spokesmen emerged on the scene to carry forth the struggle. President Grant assailed the parochial school system; but it was Rutherford B. Hayes, running for governor of Ohio, who brought forth what was to be a frequent charge: the Democratic Party had become identified with these undesirables and had in fact fallen subservient to Rome. While James Garfield blamed the 1877 riots on foreign radicals, a clergyman, speaking on behalf of the Republican national candidates in 1884, labeled the Democratic Party as the party of "Rum, Romanism, and Rebellion." Then in 1886 came the Haymarket Affair, and this ignited a nativistic feeling that reached hysterical proportions.

It was in the following year at Clinton, Iowa, that Henry F. Bowers was instrumental in the formation of the American Protective Association, the most important organized expression of anti-Catholic sentiment in the later part of the nineteenth century. Claiming that the mayor of Clinton had been defeated in his re-election bid by the Irish vote, this new organization developed along the lines of a secret, oath-bound society, similar to the then popular fraternal lodges. Included in one of its oaths is this declaration:

I hereby declare that I am a firm believer in a Deity. I am not a member of the Roman Catholic Church, nor have I any sympathy with Roman Catholicism: that in my opinion no Roman Catholic should be allowed any part or parcel in the control, or occupy any position in our public schools. On the contrary, I realize that the institutions of our country are in danger from the machinations of the Church of Rome. I believe that only by the removal of Roman Catholics from offices of trust can JUSTICE, RIGHT, and TRUE AMERICAN SENTIMENT be fully subserved; and that by the concerted and continued efforts of the lovers of American liberty only can such results be consummated and continued.

The A.P.A. also sought to curb immigration and to frustrate Roman Catholic efforts to gain public funds for parochial school purposes and further claimed as one of its purposes the liberation of the Catholic laity from blind obedience to the Church. What success it did have was in the whipping up of anti-Catholic sentiment, primarily in the rural Midwest, where the Catholic population was not heavy. Though it gained thousands of members in a very short time, primarily from among those economically threatened by the waves of immigrants in a time of embittered class conflict and social and economic frustration, and had some influence in several city and some state governments, it accomplished almost nothing in terms of actual political or legislative action. Even the publishing of a false encyclical supposedly detailing a "Popish Plot" at the time that Pope Leo XIII sent a representative to the Parliament of Religions in Chicago in 1893 did no more than fan the flames a little. The demise of the A.P.A. occurred rapidly after its secret character was made public in 1893, and then following the campaign of 1896, when the organization was split over trying to prevent the nomination of the devoutly Methodist William McKinley by the Republicans on the grounds that he was under Roman Catholic influence.

Another wave of anti-Catholic propaganda occurred from 1908 until the outbreak of World War I. A periodical, "The Menace," had a circulation of nearly one-and-a-half million by 1914. This outburst was probably prompted by the appointment of two more American cardinals, and the convening of the first American Catholic missionary conference in Chicago in 1908. The war temporarily brought an end to these hostilities, but in the 1920s they were renewed, and led to even more unfortunate incidents than in the previous fifty years.

Sometimes allied with anti-Catholicism was the issue of Sabbath observance. By the closing decades of the nineteenth century the long honored Puritan Sabbath was being seriously challenged by the Continental Sabbath. To those who held that the day was to be observed in a regimented practice of worship and quiet, the Continental Sabbath of Roman Catholicism and German Lutheranism with its practice of worship in the morning followed by boisterous relaxation, amusements and even drinking was seen as anathema to the Anglo-Saxon Protestant, albeit, American, way of life. Protestant ministers decried that the practice of purchasing Sunday newspapers, attending ball games, going on excursions, or engaging in a whole array of recreational activities was undermining the religious pillars of American society. Josiah Strong stated that "most foreigners bring with them continental ideas of the Sabbath, and the result is sadly manifest in all our cities, where it is being transformed from a holy day into a holiday." Mark Twain's character, Philip Sterling, perceived of the old-stock Americans that "temperance and the strict observance of Sunday and a certain gravity of deportment are geographical habits, which people do not usually carry with them away from home," as the rural and small town youth moved to the cities. In spite of campaigns for national legislation to preserve the old ways, many of the Sunday blue laws were in fact repealed, showing that the secularization of Sunday had a strong American base as well. When World War I came, it was deemed necessary to keep the war plants in operation on Sundays; and after that time there were far less protests over the secularization of Sunday.

The crusade occurring in the fifty years following the Civil War that gathered all others into its arms, as had the abolition movement prior to that War, was the temperance movement. This grand crusade climaxed on January 16, 1919, when national prohibition was established by the ratification of the Eighteenth Amendment. So successful was this campaign that only two states, Connecticut and Rhode Island, failed to ratify. The following year the Volstead Act defined the illegal beverages as those containing more than half of one percent of alcohol.

During the early years of the nineteenth century, American Protestantism had become more and more concerned with temperance. With the ready availability of poor quality intoxicants on the rough and lonely frontier, the denominations witnessed the severe debilitating effects of drinking. Then as revivalism became so integral to much of Protestantism, the religious awakenings they produced brought about a new piety and asceticism that emphasized a new austerity in private morality that included abstention from such worldly pleasures as drink; and also by accenting personal conversion as the central fact of religious experience, Protestantism came to oppose anything that interfered with this experience, and nothing seemed more obstructive than the curse of drink. Thus, Protestant churches appealed for temperance in individuals and developed ecclesiastical legislation to promote discipline within the churches.

The accent on individual salvation was only part of the problem caused by intemperance; for intemperance also interfered with the development of social morality as well. The result of drink was often seen in wretched homes, pauperism, crime, disease and a general lowering of the moral tone of society in general.

In dealing with this problem, as was true in other reforms as well, evangelical Protestantism sought to overcome the corruption in a dynamic manner not only by personal persuasion or ecclesiastical code, but also by Christianizing the social order through the power and force of law. Though prohibited from doing the latter directly in a land where the separation of church and state was established by law, the churches did become agents which inculcated within large numbers of its members their responsibility as Christian men and women to work through the political channels for the accomplishment of the will of God. This was initially seen in the drives for local and state option laws.

Also important in this crusade is that it was largely a middle class effort, wherein the Protestant Christian shared with his nonchurchgoing countrymen the devotion to the American ideal that all men have an equal right to life, liberty and the pursuit of happiness. For many of these this meant also that the virtue of sobriety was necessary along with honesty, industry and thrift to secure the foundation of economic success, the middle class dream. It was shown that drinking lowered a person's efficiency, and also hampered his production so that he could not take part in the economic success which was asserted as God's desire for him. Thus, "in a society where nearly everyone possessed or aspired to middle-class respectability, where material prosperity and success were regarded as evidence of virtue and marks of divine favor, and where poverty and failure were considered as probable symptoms of vice, intemperance naturally came to be viewed with stern disapproval and sobriety with high esteem."[2]

The challenge to evangelical Protestantism and middle class economic ideals presented by the industrial and urban challenge after the Civil War provided the fertile ground for the prohibition movement, as had the cheap frontier liquor of the early nineteenth century. The liquor question quickly rose again as one of major importance. This was due also in part to the rise of the liquor industry with its vast financial resources attained by the ever present saloon in the teeming cities, and by its alliance with commercialized vice and machine politicians. Josiah Strong noted "that out of 1,002 primary and other political meetings held in New York during the year preceding the November election of 1884, 633 were held in saloons and 96 were held next door to saloons, while only 283 were held apart from them." He also noted that "in 1883, of the twenty-four alderman of the city...ten were liquor dealers and two others, including the President of the Board, were ex-rumsellers." The charge was made that not only did the liquor interests buy politicians, but also aggressively undermined the urban masses, many of them recent immigrants, by seeking to provide them with the only outlet for their emotions in the cramped urban ghettos.

This was then dramatized in the evangelical Protestant mind when it was determined that only by a religious revival could America be saved, even from its urban blight; and only if the liquor problem were controlled could such a revival of religion take place. Thus with great fervor most Protestants promoted the prohibition crusade. Though the revival success was not really achieved, the Protestant churches enjoyed unprecedented success in promoting legislative reform.

The successes at legislation before the Civil War were reduced by the end of that conflict to only Maine and Massachusetts being in the dry fold, and Massachusetts soon withdrew. To recoup the losses sustained, the Grand Lodge of Good Templars launched the Prohibition party in 1869. Gaining attention only slowly, it never did become strong. The truly effective revival of the crusade against liquor began in 1874 with the formation of the Women's Christian Temperance Union. This followed a widely publicized series of demonstrations in Hillsboro, Ohio, when on Christmas Eve, 1873, more than seventy determined women left a prayer meeting and went to one of the town's liquor vendors. Without violence, but observed by hundreds, they prayed, sang, and pleaded on one side of the swinging doors or the other for the proprietor to close. During the following days they dealt in the same fashion with the twelve other saloons in the town, and achieved almost complete, though impermanent, success. The resulting WCTU significantly advanced the cause of prohibition, both by persuasion and legislation. Becoming president of the organization in 1881, Frances Willard began to implement her own ideas: a vigorous membership campaign, endless speaking tours to propagate the cause, spectacular annual conventions, and a broadening of the concerns of the WCTU to include a wide range of women's rights. She also was concerned to develop diverse political strategies to accomplish these varied goals, and became an expert practitioner of the art of pressure politics. Yet she also kept the organization firmly planted within the orbit of evangelical Protestantism. After her death in 1898, the WCTU became for all practical purposes the woman's auxiliary of a new prohibition organism, the Anti-Saloon League.

The Anti-Saloon League of America was organized in Oberlin, Ohio, in 1893 as a church-oriented direct action political pressure agency, and two years later achieved a national stature. Unlike the WCTU, the League had only one objective: to get dry laws, the drier the better; and the more stringent and sweeping the better yet. Clearly the emphasis had shifted from temperance to total abstinence to a full-scale attack upon the saloon. At this time only five of the forty-five states had adopted statewide prohibition laws, while others had made some provision for local option. The League with financial support to the tune of over $35 million by 1918 had paid agents in nearly every state and an efficient staff in the national office. Caring little about a politician's morals, so long as he voted dry, it used hard-driving, tough-minded methods that worked. The success of this drive was that it achieved the support of the old-stock middle class element in the cities and the rural and small town population, both groups being under Protestant influence and concerned with ridding the cities of vice, crime and poverty. Whether political liberals or conservatives, they jumped on the band wagon, and this then became the great Protestant

Crusade. By 1916 two-thirds of the states had taken action favorable to the dry cause, so that three-fourths of the American people lived under some kind of prohibition law.

Not all of the Protestant churches supported the League, which claimed to be: "the churches organized to fight the saloon." The Episcopal Church and the Lutheran Churches with heavy German constituencies never joined the cause, and in fact were not in sympathy with the entire religious direction of evangelical Protestantism in America. Roman Catholicism was divided over the issue. Some of the major leaders, like Archbishop John Ireland of St. Paul, endorsed the crusade; but in the main, Roman Catholics saw this as not integral to their religious way of thinking, and an attack upon their social way of life. The League enjoyed the support of most American Protestants and some Roman Catholics, but was primarily supported by the Methodists, Baptists and Presbyterians, three of the four largest members of the American Protestant community.

The social gospel writer, Charles Sheldon, came out strongly against the saloon in *In His Steps*. The main character, the Rev. Henry Maxwell, says, after passing the saloons in the Rectangle, the slum area of the city: "I have thought lately as never before of what Christian people might do to remove the curse of the saloon. Why don't we all act together against it? Why don't the Christian pastors and the church members of Raymond move as one man against the traffic? What would Jesus do? Would He keep silent? Would He vote to license these causes of crime and death?" Already in the narrative Mr. Edward Norman, who had taken the pledge never to say or do anything without first asking the question "What would Jesus do?" had decided that in his newspaper: "he would do all in his power to fight the saloon as an enemy of the human race and an unnecessary part of our civilization." As the novel proceeds, a political fight against the saloon in Raymond is undertaken by concerned Christians, but as this is in 1896 the outcome of the hotly

contested election is a triumph for the saloon forces. In the
riotous scene that precedes the announcement of the vote,
Maxwell is walking with some of his friends through the area
of the town's heaviest concentration of saloons when suddenly
a bottle is tossed down into the crowd killing one of the former
inhabitants of that area who had recently been converted. As
an epilogue to this scene Sheldon speaks out: "O Christian
America, who killed this woman? Stand back! Silence, there!
A woman has been killed. Who? Loreen. Child of the streets.
Poor, drunken, vile sinner. O Lord God, how long, how
long? Yes. The saloon killed her; that is, the Christians of
America, who license the saloon. And the Judgement Day
only shall declare who was the murderer of Loreen." Walter
Rauschenbusch also called for the churches to undertake a
temperance crusade; but one of the most flamboyant speak-
ers for prohibition was Billy Sunday, whose "booze sermon"
was a high point of his revival campaigns. Next to his passion
for the conversion of men and women was his consuming
antagonism to rum.

Setting the mood for the "booze" sermon was this hymn,
or rather, battle-cry:

> *Oh, de Brewer's big hosses, comin' down de road,*
> *Totin' all around ole Lucifer's load;*
> *Dey step so high, an' dey step so free,*
> *But dem big hosses can't run over me.*

> *Chorus:*
> *Oh, no! boys, oh, no!*
> *De turnpike's free whereebber I go,*
> *I'm a temperance ingine, doen't you see,*
> *And de Brewer's big hosses can't run over me.*

> *Oh, de licker men's actin' like dey own dis place,*
> *Livin' on de sweat ob de po' man's face,*
> *Dey's fat and sassy as dey can be,*
> *But dem big hosses can't run over me.*

Oh, I'll harness dem hosses to de temp'rance cart,
Hit 'em wid a gad to gib 'em a start,
I'll teach 'em how for to haw and gee,
For dem big hosses can't run over me.

In the sermon, Sunday made the point that the liquor industry had no interest in what its product did to the life of the
drinker, but was solely interested in the enormous profits it
made. "That is the attitude of the liquor traffic toward the
Church, and State, and Government, and the preacher that
has the backbone to fight the most damnable, corrupt institution that ever wriggled out of hell and fastened itself on the
public," had a hard job ahead of him. Yet, Sunday was con-
fident that a reform spirit was in the air, and this individual
and social curse would be eradicated. "You might as well try
and dam Niagara Falls with toothpicks as to stop the reform
wave sweeping our land," he proclaimed. He then went on to
show through an extensive use of statistics how much of the
nation's wealth was spent on the liquor trade, not only in the
purchasing of the drink, but in the cost to the public to care
for those directly and indirectly affected by the curse. He
continued by pointing out: "Seventy-five per cent of our
idiots come from the intemperate parents; eighty per cent of
the paupers, eighty-two per cent of the crime is committed by
men under the influence of liquor; ninety per cent of the adult
criminals are whiskey made." Giving individual illustrations
he played on the audiences' attachment for mother, wife and
child in depicting the suffering that befalls them because of
drinking men, especially young men. Then he stated: "The
saloon is a liar. It promises good cheer and sends sorrow. It
promises health and causes disease. It promises prosperity
and sends adversity. It promises happiness and sends misery.
Yes, it sends the husband home with a lie on his lips to his
wife; and the boy home with a lie on his lips to his mother;
and it causes the employee to lie to his employer. It degrades.
It is God's worst enemy and the devil's best friend. It spares
neither youth nor age. It is waiting with a dirty blanket for

the baby to crawl into the world. It lies in wait for the unborn." In a moment of unrestrained denunciation he blurted out: "If all the combined forces of hell should assemble in a conclave, and with them all the men on earth that hate and despise God, and purity, and virture—if all the scum of the earth could mingle with the denizens of hell to try to think of the deadliest institution to home, to church and state, I tell you, sir, the combined hellish intelligence could not conceive of or bring an institution that could touch the hem of the garment of the open licensed saloon to damn the home and manhood, and womanhood, and business and every other good thing on God's earth."

As the solution to this problem, Sunday was explicit: "Whenever the day comes that all the Catholic and Protestant churches—just when the day comes when you will say to the whiskey business: 'You go to hell,' that day the whiskey business will go to hell." He knew that day was not yet at hand, and this was because not all saw the seriousness of the problem. He declared of church leadership: "But you sit there, you old whiskey-voting elder and deacon and vestryman, and you wouldn't strike your hands together on the proposition. It would stamp you an old hypocrite and you know it." As for Sunday: "I propose to perpetuate this feud against the liquor traffic until the white-winged dove of temperance builds her nest on the dome of the capitol of Washington and spreads her wings of peace, sobriety and joy over our land which I love with all my heart." Thus he challenged his hearers: "You men have a chance to show your manhood. Then in the name of your pure mother, in the name of your manhood, in the name of your wife and the poor innocent children that climb up on your lap and put their arms around your neck, in the name of all that is good and noble, fight the curse. Shall you men, who hold in your hands the ballot, and in that ballot hold the destiny of womanhood and childhood and manhood, shall you, the sovereign power, refuse to rally in the name of the defenseless men and women and native land? No."

Realizing that he was not reaching those captive of the saloon, Sunday joined with others in making his appeal to the middle-class voters to take the necessary corrective action. In 1913 this took the form of a campaign for an amendment to the Constitution. When the congressional election of 1914 was over a dry majority had been seated. Then came the War with its resultant rationale for harassing German brewers, and then after America's entrance into the conflict the cause was furthered by the stress laid on saving fuel (alcohol) and using grain for bread. On December 18, 1917, the Eighteenth Amendment cleared the House 282 to 128 and with tremendous speed received the necessary ratification by the state legislatures. The Great Crusade had been accomplished, and the effort had united Protestant Americans as nothing else ever had, and still today has left a tangible residue in many communities; and most certainly in most Protestant churches, which holding theologically to a memorial or symbolical understanding of the Lord's Supper, use unfermented grape juice, rather than wine, in the sacramental observance.

Expressive of the interdenominational cooperation that the prohibition crusade exemplified, as did the foreign mission and Sunday school movements, was the formation of the Federal Council of the Churches of Christ in America in 1908. This was the outgrowth of numerous endeavors such as the mid-nineteenth century Evangelical Alliance to bring the highly institutionally fragmented American Protestant scene into a medium of common action. The twenty-eight denominations which had approved this organization prior to the 1908 meeting did not dissolve their separate identities, but were expressing a rising conviction on the part of American Protestants that some type of confederation which made possible particular co-ordinated actions was indeed needed. The pitfalls of theological dispute were largely avoided by agreeing not to discuss theological matters, but rather to be concerned with areas of agreed need in "applied Christianity." The Council was to meet quadrennially to pursue its stated objectives:

I.   To express the fellowship and catholic unity of the Christian Church.
II. To bring the Christian bodies of America into united service for Christ and the world.
III. To encourage devotional fellowship and mutual counsel concerning the spiritual life and religious activities of the Churches.
IV. To secure a larger combined influence for the Churches of Christ in all matters affecting the moral and social condition of the people, so as to promote the application of the law of Christ in every relation to human life. [3]

Called a marriage of the ecumenical movement and the social gospel, the Federal Council hoped to be the agency whereby the crusading spirit of American Protestantism might be funneled to secure the greatest good. The denominations participating, representing a rather broad perspective of American religion, believed that they lived in a great age and had a rare opportunity to enlarge and enhance the reign of God in His kingdom on earth. It was for these churches to be now about the concrete task of bringing this into being. At that 1908 meeting the Social Creed of the Churches that had been developed by the Methodist Church was adopted as tangible evidence of the Federal Council's determination to take action with regard to this major social problem of the day. In 1916 it came out in support of the Eighteenth Amendment by stating: "Total abstinence for the individual and prohibition for the state and nation is the path of wisdom and safety," so that another basic social problem facing America was addressed by a large segment of its Protestant community in unison. Other areas of basic concern were world missions, religious education, evangelism, care of the Black churches, support of needy Protestant churches in other lands, social service projects on the national scene, and encouragement of local and state federations. Not becoming a political pressure group, the Federal Council through study groups and published findings sought to clarify major issues and to seek to inform and persuade the American community about the Christian concerns for the 'advancement of our common life. In this way the crusading spirit received an institutional church structure by which to address the major problems confronting the American scene in the midst of the peak period of Protestant influence and activity in America.

The fifty years following the Civil War thus saw a continuance of the spirit of conquest that was seemingly so integral to the American experience. This crusading spirit involved not only a conquest of new geographic territories, but also consisted of determined efforts to preserve by both persuasion and legislation, and even at times by warfare, the values so widely advocated in the popular religion of the era.

Epilogue

As historians of the American religious experience survey the American scene during the decades following the Civil War, it becomes clear that in religious as well as socio-economic life, the Gilded Age was the matrix of modern America. Arthur Schlesinger, Sr. stated that during these years organized religion in the nation was challenged on two fronts: "the one to its system of thought, the other to its social program." It was the types of responses to these challenges that was largely to set the tone for the nation's religious life for years to come.

The gospel of wealth sanctified the entrepreneurial gains, so long as the triumphant remained sensitive to their duty under God to the development of society as well as industry. The social gospel represented the unique American reaction to the results of the Gilded Age, drawing its dynamics and its ideology from the social context in which it grew. Some of its advocates called for a reformation in American life to counter the mammonistic tendencies seemingly let loose by industrialization, while others clamored for religion to be the formative agent in developing a cooperative society to replace the highly competitive one that had come into being.

Many of these debates did indeed center about the new urban centers; but much of American Protestantism was here put to a severe test, as its experience in America was largely in the rural areas and small towns. In fact, this orientation was so strong that when it did seek to meet urban challenges much of Protestantism sought to do so largely on the basis of what had succeeded in these areas. Instead of articulating a faith rooted in the urban environment, much of Protestantism sought instead to steel its members so that their character would not be corroded by the urban scene. Indicative of this is the perennial revivalists calling forth the solid character of the traditional family and church life that the emigrants to the city had left behind, and also seeking to implant within them a moral code that espoused the virtues of an earlier and simpler life in pre-Civil War America.

Even the thinking with regard to denominational expansion into the arid Plains and Intermountain West was circumscribed by the institutional forms, thought patterns and mission methods that had been utilized on the grassy and humid plains of the Ohio-Mississippi River valleys. In both the new urban centers and on the wide open frontiers it was hard for mission executives and their clergy to recognize that the church as an institution was not accorded the place in society that it had in the small towns of America.

At times it was the proclamation of a crusade that led Protestants to attempt to batter down presumed enemies to what had made the earlier nineteenth century such a time of religious activity, hope and triumph. The success of some of these crusades was often very limited, but this in no way deterred the battles from being waged; while the success of others was very notable at this time, thus encouraging even more attempts to be made, especially as it was recognized that the generally accepted Protestant character of the nation was endangered, and therefore the old ways and old ideas must be preserved to prevent what Lincoln had described as the "last, best hope of earth" from being overcome. Nonetheless, it was in the Gilded Age that Protestant doctrines and symbols discernibly began to lose their hold on the American people and their dominance in the culture in general. Some of these, however, were infused with new meanings and a form of Americanism became the dominant motif that was proclaimed. This could be seen in the revivalists' call to restore the ways of the past or in the liberal theologians' accent on the developments that were occurring across the land as indicative that Americans were coming to a greater and greater awareness of the immanence of God in their midst.

It was in the Roman Catholic Church, so largely located in the industrial centers, that is seen the determined effort to address the economic and social as well as religious needs of the seemingly unending stream of immigrants. This may have even been a struggle for survival as these immigrants and their children had to have a sympathetic church attuned to their needs if they were to retain their religious affiliation. The Church did not turn its back on these people, and moreover, ministered to them relevently in their urban situations. The Jewish story was much the same, except that for Catholicism the ubiquitous parochial school passed from one generation to the next the integrity of the faith, while in the Jewish community this was lost as the young were instructed in Americanism in the public schools so that their Jewishness became an ethnic more than a religious identity.

Statistically, the half century following the Civil War was a time of phenomenal institutional expansion. C.C. McCabe of the Methodist Church Extension Society could respond to the taunts of the popular atheist, Robert Ingersoll, by sending him a telegram reading: "Dear Robert: 'All Hail the power of Jesus' name'—we are building more than one Methodist Church for every day in the year, and propose to make it two a day!" Showing the need for such building campaigns was the fact that between 1865 and 1917 Protestant church membership reputedly rose from five million to twenty-three million, while during the same period the Roman Catholic constituency rose from three-and-a-half million to eighteen million; whereas less than twenty per cent of the population was formally connected to a church in 1865, more than forty per cent had such an affiliation in 1917, even as the nation's population had more than tripled.

The story of this half century is a story of successes and of failures for the religious forces of the nation; yet the end result is that with numerical success but with substance often eroded, religion had indeed made an impact on American life, but had now to face the difficult decades which followed World War I.

References

1. Sidney Mead, *The Lively Experiment: The Shaping of Christianity in America.* (New York: Harper & Row, 1963), p. 135.

2. *Ibid.*

3. *Ibid.*

4. Quoted in Sidney Ashlstrom, *A Religious History of the American People.* (New Haven: Yale University Press, 1972), pp. 728-729.

5. E. Franklin Frazier, *The Negro Church in America* (New York: Schocken Books, 1973), p. 34.

6. *Ibid.*, pp. 45-46.

7. Mead, *The Lively Experiment*, p. 169.

8. Bert J. Lowenberg, *Darwinism Comes to America: 1859-1900.* (Philadelphia: Fortress Press, 1969), p. 5.

9. *Ibid.*, p. 6.

10. Ernest R. Sandeen, *The Origins of Fundamentalism.* (Philadelphia: Fortress Press, 1968), p. 4.

11. *Ibid.*, p. 8.

12. Mead, *The Lively Experiment*, p. 143.

13. Paul A. Carter, *The Spiritual Crisis of the Gilded Age.* (Dekalb, Ill.: Northern Illinois University Press, 1972), p. 130.

Chapter II: The Industrial Challenge

1. Mead, *The Lively Experiment*, p. 101.

2. Henry F. May, *Protestant Churches and Industrial America* (New York: Harper & Row, 1967), p. 91.

3. Robert T. Handy, *A Christian America: Protestant Hopes and Historical Realities.* (New York: Oxford University Press, 1971), p. 157.

Chapter III: The Urban Impact

1. Josiah Strong, *Our Country*. (Cambridge: Belknap Press of Harvard University Press, 1963), p. 171.

2. Quoted in Winthrop Hudson, *The Great Tradition of the American Churches*. (New York: Harper & Brothers, 1953), p. 132.

3. Gerald Shaughnessy, *Has the Immigrant Kept the Faith? A Study of Immigration and Catholic Growth in the United States, 1790-1920*. New York: Macmillan, 1925.

Chapter IV: Campaigns for the Soul

1. Quoted in Gamaliel Bradford, *D.L. Moody: A Worker in Souls*. (New York: George H. Doran, 1927), p. 16.

2. William G. McLoughlin, Jr. *Modern Revivalism: Charles Grandison Finney to Billy Graham*. (New York: Ronald Press, 1959), p. 262.

3. *Ibid.*, p. 336.

4. *Ibid.*, p. 346.

5. William T. Ellis, *"Billy" Sunday: The Man and His Message*. (Philadelphia: John C. Winton Co., 1914), p. 70.

6. McLoughlin, *Modern Revivalism*, p. 445.

Chapter V: Westward Ho!

1. Quoted in Winfred Garrison, *The March of Faith*. (New York: Harper & Brothers, 1933), p. 51.

2. William N. Sloan, *Spiritual Conquest Along the Rockies*. (New York: Hodder and Stoughton, 1913), pp. 83-84.

3. C.B. Evans, *Another Montana Pioneer*. (privately printed, 1960), p. 114.

4. Montana Methodist Messenger, XVI (August, 1920) p. 6.

Chapter VI: The Crusading Spirit

1. Garrison, *March of Faith*, p. 138.

2. James H. Timberlake, *Prohibition and the Progressive Movement 1900-1920*. (Cambridge: Harvard University Press, 1963), p. 9.

3. Quoted in Jerald C. Brauer, *Protestantism in America: A Narrative History*, rev. ed. (Philadelphia: Westminster Press, 1965), p. 250.

Suggested Readings

General Works on the American Scene

Graff, Henry F. gen. ed. *The Life History of the United States.* Vols. 6-9 New York: Time Incorporated, 1963-1964.

Williams, T. Harry. *The Union Restored.* (1861-1876)

Weisberger, Bernard A. *The Age of Steel and Steam.* (1877-1890)

_____. *Reaching for Empire.* (1890-1901)

May, Ernest R. *The Progressive Era.* (1901-1917)

See also:

Clemens, Samuel L. and Warner, Charles D. *The Gilded Age: A Tale of Today.* Vols. 10-11. *The Writings of Mark Twain, pseud.* New York: Harper & Brothers, 1906.

Curti, Merle. *The Growth of American Thought.* 3rd ed. New York: Harper & Row, 1964.

Gabriel, Ralph H. *The Course of American Democratic Thought.* 2nd. ed. New York: Ronald Press, 1956.

Hoogenboom, Ari and Hoogenboom, Olive. eds. *The Gilded Age.* Englewood Cliffs, N.J.: Prentice-Hall, 1967.

General Works on American Religious History

Ahlstrom, Sidney. *A Religious History of the American People.* New Haven: Yale University Press, 1972.

Brauer, Jerald C. *Protestantism in America: A Narrative History.* rev. ed. Philadelphia: Westminster Press, 1965.

Ellis, John T. *American Catholicism.* 2nd ed., rev. Chicago: University of Chicago Press.

Garrison, Winfred E. *The March of Faith.* New York: Harper and Brothers, 1933.

Handy, Robert T. ed. *Religion in the American Experience.* New York: Harper & Row, 1972.

Hudson, Winthrop. *The Great Tradition of the American Churches.* New York: Harper and Brothers, 1953.

_____. *Religion in America.* 2nd. ed. New York: Charles Scribner's Sons, 1973.

Marty, Martin E. *Righteous Empire: The Protestant Experience in America.* New York: Dial Press, 1970.

Mead, Sidney E. *The Lively Experiment: The Shaping of Christianity in America.* New York: Harper & Row, 1963.

Olmstead, Clifton E. *History of Religion in the United States.* Englewood Cliffs, N.J.: Prentice-Hall, 1960.

Smith, H. Sheldon, Handy, Robert T. and Loetscher, Lefferts A. *American Christianity: An Historical Interpretation with Representative Documents.* Vol. II (1820-1960). New York: Charles Scribner's Sons, 1963.

See also for the most complete bibliography on American religious history:

Burr, Nelson R. *A Critical Bibliography in Religion* in Smith, J. Ward and Jamison, A. Leland, eds. *Religion in American Life.* 4 vols. Princeton: Princeton University Press, 1961.

Chapter I: Theological Currents

Abbott, Lyman. *Henry Ward Beecher.* Boston: Houghton, Mifflin & Co., 1904.

_____. *Theology of an Evolutionist.* Boston: Houghton, Mifflin & Co., 1897.

Braden, Charles S. *These Also Believe: A Study of Modern American Cults and Minority Religious Movements.* New York: Macmillan, 1949.

Clark, Elmer T. *The Small Sects in America.* rev. ed. Nashville: Abingdon Press, 1949.

Foster, Frank H. *The Modern Movement in American Theology: Sketches in the History of American Protestant Thought from the Civil War to the World War.* New York: Fleming H. Revell, 1939.

Gottschalk, Stephen. *The Emergence of Christian Science in American Religious Life.* Berkeley: University of California Press, 1974.

Hofstadter, Richard. *Social Darwinism in American Thought.* rev. ed. Boston: Beacon Press, 1955.

Hutchinson, William R. ed. *American Protestant Thought: The Liberal Era.* New York: Harper and Row, 1968.

Judah, J. Stillson. *The History and Philosophy of the Metaphysical Movements in America.* Philadelphia: Westminter Press, 1957.

Mays, Benjmin E. & Nicolson, Joseph W. *The Negro's Church.* New York: Institute of Social and Religious Research, 1933.

McGiffert, Arthur C. *The Rise of Modern Religious Ideas,* New York: Macmillan Co., 1915.

Nelson, E. Clifford, ed. *The Lutherans in North America.* Philadelphia: Fortress Press, 1975.

Chapter II: The Industrial Challenge

Conwell, Russell. *Acres of Diamonds.* Lexington, Ky.: Successful Achievement, 1971.

Handy, Robert T. ed. *The Social Gospel in America, 1870-1920.* New York: Oxford University Press, 1966.

Hopkins, Charles H. *The Rise of the Social Gospel in American Protestantism, 1865-1915.* New Haven: Yale University Press, 1940.

Kennedy, Gail, ed. *Democracy and the Gospel of Wealth.* Boston: D.C. Heath, 1949.

Kirkland, Edward C. ed. *The Gospel of Wealth, and other timely essays.* Cambridge: Belknap Press of Harvard University Press, 1965.

Landis, Benson Y., ed. *A Rauschenbusch Reader: The King-dom of God and the Social Gospel.* New York: Harper and Brothers, 1957.

Rauschenbush, Walter. *Christianity and the Social Crisis.* New York: Macmillan, 1907.

_____. *Christianizing the Social Order.* New York: Macmillan, 1913.

_____. *A Theology for the Social Gospel.* New York: Macmillan, 1917.

Schlesinger, Arthur M., Sr. *A Critical Period in American Religion.* Philadelphia: Fortress Press, 1967.

Sheldon, Charles M. *In His Steps.* (numerous editions)

Chapter III: The Urban Impact

Abell, Aaron I. *The Urban Impact on American Protestantism 1865-1900.* Cambridge: Harvard University Press, 1943.

Cross, Robert D. *The Church and the City, 1865-1910.* Indianapolis: Bobbs-Merrill Co., 1967.

Glazer, Nathan. *American Judaism.* Chicago: University of Chicago Press, 1957.

Handlin, Oscar. *The Uprooted: The Epic Story of the Great Migrations that Made the American People.* Boston: Little, Brown and Co., 1951.

Hopkins, Charles H. *A History of the Y.M.C.A. in North America.* New York: Association Press, 1951.

Meltzer, Milton. *Remember the Days.* Garden City, N.Y.: Doubleday, 1974.

Riis, Jacob A. *How the Other Half Lives; studies among the tenements of New York.* New York: Charles Scribner's Sons, 1912.

Roemer, Theodore. *The Catholic Church in the United States.* St. Louis: Herder Book Co., 1950.

Wisbey, Herbert A., Jr. *Soldier's Without Swords: A History of the Salvation Army in the United States.* New York: Macmillan, 1955.

Chapter IV: Campaigns for the Soul

Findlay, James F., Jr. *Dwight L. Moody: American Evangelist, 1837-1899*. Chicago: University of Chicago Press, 1969.

McLoughlin, William G., Jr. *Billy Sunday Was His Real Name*. Chicago: University of Chicago Press, 1955.

Moody, William R. *The Life of Dwight L. Moody*. Chicago: Fleming H. Revell, 1900.

Weisberger, Bernard A. *They Gathered at the River; the story of the Revivalists and their Impact upon Religion in America*. Boston: Little, Brown & Co., 1958.

Chapter V: Westward Ho!

Fogde, Myron J., "Protestantism in Frontier Montana" unpublished Ph.D. dissertation, University of Chicago, 1963.

Goodykoontz, Colin B., *Home Missions on the American Frontier, with particular reference to the American Home Missionary Society*. Caldwell, Id. Caxton Printers, 1939.

Lind, Robert W., *From the Ground Up: The Story of Brother Van, Montana Pioneer Minister, 1847-1919*. Helena, Mt.: Treasure State Publishing, 1961.

Mills, Edward L., *Plains, Peaks and Pioneers: Eighty Years of Methodism in Montana*. Portland: Binfords and Mort, 1947.

Rolvaag, Ole E., *Giants in the Earth*. New York: Harper and Brothers, 1929.

Tuttle, Daniel S., *Reminiscences of a Missionary Bishop*. New York: Thomas Whittaker, 1906.

Chapter VI: The Crusading Spirit

Cherry, Conrad, ed. *God's New Israel: Religious Interpretations of American Destiny*. New York: Prentice-Hall, 1971.

Kinzer, Donald L., *An Episode in Anti-Catholicism, The American Protective Association*. Seattle: University of Washington Press, 1964.

Macfarland, Charles S., *Christian Unity in the Making: The First Twenty-five Years of the Federal Council of the*

Churches of Christ in America, 1905-1930. New York: Federal Council of Churches of Christ in America, 1948.

Mott, John R., *The Evangelization of the World in This Generation.* New York: Student Volunteer Movement, 1900.